The Catholic Biblical School Program

# YEAR FOUR

# THE OLD AND NEW TESTAMENTS CONCLUDED: THE WORD IN THE HELLENISTIC WORLD

## STUDENT WORKBOOK

Prepared by
A. Gene Giuliano, Jr., Judith A. Hubert, Dorothy Jonaitis, and Brian Schmisek

PAULIST PRESS
New York/Mahwah, NJ

**Acknowledgements**
The Publisher gratefully acknowledges use of the following materials: Excerpts from *Ancient Near Eastern Texts*, edited by James B. Pritchard, copyright © 1969, Princeton University Press; excerpts from "Why Do Christians Have Different Bibles?" by Brother Daniel F. Stramara, OSB, from *Pecos Newsletter* and appearing also as Dove Leaflet no. 102; excerpts from *Introduction to Old Testament Wisdom* by Anthony Ceresko, copyright ©1999, Orbis Books (Maryknoll, NY); "Four Ways to Follow Jesus" by Steve Mueller, originally published by St. Anthony Messenger Press (Cincinnati, OH) as Catholic Update C1292.

Special thanks to Mary Ingenthron and Mary Kay Swenson for the biblical drawings that are included throughout this book.



Cover design by Sharyn Banks

Book design by Celine Allen

*Nihil Obstat:* Rev. Msgr. Robert M. Coerver, V.F.
*Censor Librorum*

*Imprimatur:* + Most Reverend Kevin J. Farrell, D.D.
*Bishop of Dallas*

October 1, 2009

The *Nihil Obstat* and *Imprimatur* are official declarations that the material reviewed contains nothing contrary to Faith and Morals. It is not implied thereby that those granting the *Nihil Obstat* and *Imprimatur* agree with the contents, statements, or opinions expressed.



ISBN: 978-0-8091-9590-9

Published by Paulist Press
997 Macarthur Boulevard
Mahwah, New Jersey 07430
www.paulistpress.com

Printed and bound in the United States of America

# Dedication

It is with respect and gratitude that this revision of *The Denver Catholic Biblical School Program* is dedicated to Sister Macrina Scott, OSF. It was her recognition of the need for a serious Bible study for the Catholic laity that led to the creation of the Catholic Biblical School in 1982. As the founder and for twenty years director of the school, Sister Macrina is a leader in the area of adult Catholic biblical literacy. We are grateful to her for the great gift that she has given to the church.

Because of her vision and determination, literally thousands of Catholics have had their eyes and hearts opened to the word and have grown in faith and knowledge, deepening their relationship with God through their study of scripture. With the publication of the Biblical School materials by Paulist Press beginning in 1994, Sister Macrina's dream bore fruit throughout the country. It is our hope that these revisions, renamed *The Catholic Biblical School Program*, will keep that dream alive well into the twenty-first century.

In addition, we would be remiss not to acknowledge the significant contributions of Steve Mueller, PhD, to the development of the original Biblical School program. We remember Mary E. Ingenthron, now deceased, whose delightful illustrations grace this book. Finally, we thank our own CBS Dallas graduate Mary Kay Swenson who created drawings for lessons which previously had none.

# Contents


Foreword ..... vii

Introduction ..... ix

**Unit I: Wisdom in Israel ..... 1**

I.1 INTRODUCTION TO WISDOM LITERATURE ..... 2
I.2 THE BEAUTY OF WISDOM: PROVERBS 1-9 ..... 4
I.3 WISDOM IN CULTURAL CONTEXTS: PROVERBS 10, 16, 22-24, 28, 30-31 ..... 6
I.4 WISDOM CHALLENGED—GOD ON TRIAL: HABAKKUK; JOB 1-14, 42:7-17 ..... 8
I.5 WISDOM CHALLENGED—GOD ON TRIAL: JOB 19, 28-32, 36:22—42:17 ..... 10
I.6 THE FAILURE OF WISDOM: ECCLESIASTES (QOHELETH) ..... 12
I.7 WISDOM REAFFIRMED: SIRACH (ECCLESIASTICUS) 1-4, 14-18, 20-23 ..... 14
I.8 WISDOM REAFFIRMED: SIRACH (ECCLESIASTICUS) 24-26, 30, 34, 38-39, 42-51 ..... 16
I.9 WISDOM REVISED: THE BOOK OF WISDOM (WISDOM OF SOLOMON) ..... 18
I.10 UNIT ONE REVIEW ..... 20

**Unit II: Judaism in the Hellenistic World ..... 21**

II.1 JONAH ..... 22
II.2 ESTHER ..... 24
II.3 TOBIT ..... 26
II.4 BARUCH ..... 28
II.5 1 MACCABEES ..... 30
II.6 2 MACCABEES ..... 32
II.7 JUDITH ..... 34
II.8 DANIEL 1-6, 13-14 ..... 36
II.9 DANIEL 7-12 ..... 38
II.10 UNIT TWO REVIEW ..... 40

**Unit III: Early Christian Development ..... 41**

III.1 MATTHEW 1-4 ..... 42
III.2 MATTHEW 5-7 ..... 44
III.3 MATTHEW 8-10 ..... 46
III.4 MATTHEW 11-17 ..... 48
III.5 MATTHEW 18-23 ..... 50
III.6 MATTHEW 24-28 ..... 52
III.7 NEW TESTAMENT LETTERS I: 1 and 2 TIMOTHY, TITUS, JAMES ..... 54
III.8 NEW TESTAMENT LETTERS II: 1 and 2 PETER, JUDE ..... 56
III.9 HEBREWS ..... 58
III.10 UNIT THREE REVIEW ..... 60

## SUPPLEMENTARY READINGS


1. The Historical Background for the Wisdom Writings: An Overview ....65
2. Wisdom in Israel: Overview ....69
3. Selections from the Instruction of Amen-em-Opet....71
4. Self-Quiz: Mid-Unit One....73
5. Why Do Christians Have Different Bibles? ....74
6. Truth and Its Many Expressions ....79
7. Judaism in the Hellenistic World: Overview....81
8. Canon Quiz ....84
9. Who's Who in Maccabees ....86
10. Self-Quiz: Mid-Unit Two ....88
11. The Three Stages of the Composition of the Gospels (Vatican II) ....89
12. The Synoptic Gospels and Their Sources....90
13. Material Usually Allotted to *Q* ....92
14. *M* Passages ....95
15. The Gospel of Matthew: Overview ....96
16. Jesus' Journey in Matthew ....98
17. Self-Quiz: Mid-Unit Three....99
18. Four Ways to Follow Jesus ....100
19. *Nostra Aetate* §4 ....106
20. The Jewish People and Their Sacred Scripture in the Christian Bible ....108
21. New Testament Writings: Overview ....111

Self-Quiz Answers....113

Four-Year Plan of Study in the Catholic Biblical School ....115

# Foreword

Welcome to The Catholic Biblical School Program. In the Catholic Church, sacred scripture is often called "the soul of theology." The study of sacred scripture on the part of Catholics reached new levels after Vatican II. Many programs have arisen since to meet that need. One was the Denver Catholic Biblical School, which was founded more than twenty-five years ago. Since that time, the program has flourished in many places throughout the United States and beyond. One reason for its success is that it incorporates the fruit of the "indispensable method" of historical criticism into the rich faith tradition of the church and the lives of the students.

As dean of the University of Dallas School of Ministry, I was elated when we were able to hire first Mr. Gene Giuliano, then Sr. Dorothy Jonaitis, OP, and finally Ms. Angeline Hubert. Each of them is an acknowledged author of the "original" Denver Catholic Biblical School program materials, and each of them taught in the school for a time. Now, as faculty members at the Catholic Biblical School of the School of Ministry, they bring significant experience to their writing.

In this revision, we have incorporated lessons learned from scholarship, from classroom teaching (our own and others'), from updated materials, including the publication of the *Catechism of the Catholic Church* and statements from the Pontifical Biblical Commission, and our own growth in spirituality and faith. We present the product of countless hours of discussion, prayer, and scholarly debate.

By using this workbook, you will become more familiar with the Bible. You will learn about its stories, its characters, its places, its themes, its promises, and its hopes. This sacred text will meet you in your own life, with your cares, concerns, worries, hopes, ambitions, and faith. The sacred is something that exhausts us. We do not exhaust it. Time and again we approach it anew, whether we are seventeen or seventy-seven. We encourage you on your path to learning more about the sacred text, its inspired character, and its primary author. We hope you will find the workbook material nourishing both academically and spiritually.

Brian Schmisek, PhD
Dean, School of Ministry
University of Dallas

# Introduction

Welcome to the fourth and final year of your spiritual journey using *The Catholic Biblical School Program*. You are now a seasoned traveler in the worlds of ancient Judaism and early Christianity because of your three years of experience in our program. Recall that in your first year, you studied the literary presentation of the historical development of the Jewish people, and in your second year the basic story of Jesus Christ and the Christian community. In your third year, you discovered the prophetic perspective on the crucial experience of exile and restoration. This year we conclude our examination of both the Old and New Testaments as we focus on *The Word in the Hellenistic World*. Most of the biblical books we study express the challenges presented to both Jews and Christians struggling to live their faith in an environment that did not share their core beliefs and values.

### A Preview of the Fourth Year Journey

In the first two units, we concentrate on the post-exilic experience of the Jewish people, especially the challenge faced by those Jews living in the Diaspora (i.e., anywhere except their Palestinian homeland). These "dispersed" Jews needed to find ways of supporting their faith without the reinforcement available in their home culture. The books we will study reflect the post-exilic challenge of living the Jewish faith in a Hellenistic culture that did not accept the Jewish beliefs or their way of life.

Many Bible study programs contain little or nothing on the wisdom literature and the other post-exilic books; this is the case particularly in non-Catholic programs that do not include some of these books in their Bibles. However, many non-Catholics are once again rediscovering these books because they provide so much material about the Jewish world in the three hundred years of Hellenistic influence before the coming of Jesus. The books take on a greater importance because they help us understand the social and cultural world in which Jesus and the first Christian communities lived.

In the first unit, "Wisdom in Israel," we read the Jewish wisdom literature. This literature is rooted in the long tradition of guidance for responsible living commonly shared by most of the ancient Near Eastern peoples. However, the Jews reflect on this tradition from the viewpoint of their post-exilic development as a renewed covenant people and so transform the tradition into one that is imbued with their specific religious beliefs. The wisdom tradition reveals an exciting and creative enterprise in Jewish theology. It attempts to bring together the general wisdom traditions, which were based on everyday experience and on the patterns of creation, with specifically Jewish traditions based on a covenant with God. This unity of both creation and covenant styles of theology is a triumph of theological thinking that still serves both Jews and Christians to this day.

In the second unit, "Judaism in the Hellenistic World," we read a variety of books that reflect the conflict between the developing Jewish style of life and that of the surrounding Hellenistic culture. The books include short fictional narratives (Jonah, Esther, Tobit, Judith), the national history written for the Maccabee rulers, and apocalyptic resistance literature (Daniel). The common element is that in one way or another the books all provided their readers with guidelines for being a Jew in Hellenistic culture. Sometimes this meant solidifying the community's identity and mission, and sometimes it meant active resistance and military rebellion against Hellenistic overlords. But always it meant recognizing who God was and what God was doing for the community. This is the core concern of all of these books.

In the third unit, "Early Christian Development," we shift to the difficulties that Christians had in the last third of the first century as they emerged from association with Judaism into their own identity in the Roman World. The Gospel of Matthew reveals the struggles of a Christian community that had to part ways with its ancestral Jewish lifestyle and commit itself to a fuller participation in the Gentile-oriented progress of the Christian Church. Through his portrait of Jesus, Matthew provides guidelines for building on the Jewish heritage yet moving outward into the primarily Gentile church of the late first century. The pastoral and catholic letters provide a good picture of the demands on the Christian communities to develop structures for survival in a non-Christian world. The letters reveal the ways in which various communities dealt with the perplexing problems of authority, leadership, doctrine, moral behavior, and community structures. Taken together they show how the early communities coped with the problem of translating their faith into community life.

**Preparing for the Fourth-Year Journey**

As you know, the most important resource for your study is your Bible. The translations recommended in your first year, the *New American Bible* (NAB), the *Revised Standard Version* (RSV) or the *New Revised Standard Version* (NRSV), and the *New Jerusalem Bible* (NJB) are all good choices. For the books of Esther and Daniel a Catholic version will be more practical as other translations have different arrangements of entire sections. The division of the biblical books into chapters and verses was done long after the text was written. There is nothing divinely inspired about these designations. Our primary chapter and verse numbers are those of the *New Revised Standard Version*. Chapter and verse numbers for the *New American Bible* and the *New Jerusalem Bible* are given in parentheses when they differ from those in the NRSV.

Once again, we encourage you to reread the Vatican II Dogmatic Constitution on Divine Revelation (*Dei Verbum*) to review the principles and norms of the Catholic Church's teaching on the nature, transmission, interpretation, and application of divine revelation. You will also find paragraphs 50–184 of the *Catechism of the Catholic Church* helpful for refreshing your understanding of God's revelation and our response of faith. As in the first three years of your study, we have suggested readings from the *Catechism* in the **Further Reading** section of each lesson.

As you read various commentaries and listen to lectures, keep in mind that there is a range of opinions among biblical scholars about such matters as literary genres, authorship, and dating of biblical writings. Time does not permit the exploration of all the various hypotheses. This workbook and the assigned readings try to present the current scholarly consensus on given questions, but we realize that alternate views are held by other reputable scholars. Since scholarly research on the Bible is always developing, we know that these positions are subject to further revision. Focus primarily on learning to read and interpret the Bible "according to the same Spirit by whom it was written" (*Dei Verbum*, §12). Learn to apply it to your life "within the living tradition of the Church, whose first concern is fidelity to the revelation attested by the Bible" (Pontifical Biblical Commission, *The Interpretation of the Bible in the Church*, [1993], III).

Once again you will be using your Eerdmans *Dictionary of the Bible* for background materials that will clarify the biblical texts and your Hammond *Atlas of the Bible Lands* that will help you find the locations of the places and events that you will study about this year.

For each unit of study, we will also recommend textbooks that we have found helpful for understanding this material. Particularly important will be Lawrence Boadt's *Reading the Old Testament* (which you used in the first and third years of our program), George Montague's *Companion God*, and Joseph Kelly's *Introduction to the New Testament* (which you used in the second year) to help you find your way through this year of studies.

There are a number of helpful books and commentaries about the wisdom literature, the deuterocanonical books, the Gospel of Matthew, and the letters we will study. We have listed many books and articles in the **Further Reading** section of each lesson. You may also check what is available through your parish or public library or any other libraries to which you have access. Your teacher can also suggest other books that might be helpful for topics that interest you.

### Making the Journey

You are already familiar with the process of making the biblical journey using our study materials. The **Geography Task** helps you situate major events in their geographic setting. The **Important Terms** direct your attention to the key concepts emphasized in each lesson. The **Written Work** leads you directly to the Bible texts that you have been assigned to read and helps you apply these texts to your life.

Each week we also provide **Optional Challenges** that require a bit more thinking and research than the basic questions. You may also find other intriguing things that you want to explore. Make these into optional challenges and share your findings with your group.

Each lesson also includes a **Memory Verse Suggestion**. You might think that memorizing these and other verses of scripture is irrelevant but these verses are a first step in making the Bible texts your own. Without some memorization, it is difficult to have scripture texts readily available for your prayer and application to the situations of your life. You will find that there are many profound and helpful verses from the prophets that you will want to make your own.

### Companions for the Journey

As you have learned from your work during previous years in the program, there is not only one teacher in the class. As adult learners you know that some of your best teachers are the people in your small group with whom you share your journey. Again this year, they will surprise you with their insights into Old and New Testament books that you will study. Just as each of the biblical authors takes a particular perspective that depends on his own experiences and circumstances, so each one in your group will have his or her special viewpoint on the material you study each week. God's word can be found and heard not just as it is encapsulated in the scripture text, but also as it is incarnated in the persons with whom you study. As always, your group sharing should be guided by:

**The Ten Commandments of Group Process**

1. Work to build trust and intimacy within your group.
2. Get to the heart of the passage. Don't just skim the surface.
3. Give everyone in your group a chance to talk. No speeches!
4. Speak connectedly with previous speakers. Consciously work at building bridges with what has already been said.
5. While one person speaks, everyone else listens.
6. Never ridicule or cut down another's answers.
7. When you disagree, do so with respect.
8. Do not fear silence.
9. If you have not completed your homework, be a participant "listener" for those questions that you have not completed.
10. Enjoy yourself!

As you have discovered from the previous three years, the journey to God through scripture brings many surprises. Students often begin this year with practically no knowledge of the wisdom literature, the deuterocanonical books, or the historical period from which they come. As their study progresses, many students are surprised at how similar many aspects of the Jewish faith are to our own. The message of the wisdom literature, the example of the characters in the deuterocanonical books, and the challenge of Matthew and the other New Testament authors take on a new relevance. These books illuminate the possibilities for faithful and wise responses to God in the complex situations of our modern world.

As we progress in our familiarity with God's Word to us, we might do well to recall often the words of the fourth-century Syrian scripture scholar St. Ephraem:

> "Lord, who can comprehend even one of your words? We lose more of it than we grasp, like those who drink from a living spring. For God's word offers different facets according to the capacity of the listener, and the Lord has portrayed the message in many colors, so that whoever gazes on it can see in it what is suitable. Within it God has buried manifold treasures, so that each of us might grow rich in seeking them out."
>
> —*Commentary on the Diatessaron*

# UNIT I
# Wisdom in Israel

**Objectives**

After completing this unit, you will be able to:

1. Recognize the distinctive sources, literary forms, and theological themes of Israel's wisdom traditions.
2. Identify the historical and social situation in which the Hebrew wisdom literature developed.
3. Apply the wisdom message to your present situation.

## Textbooks

**Primary Text:** The Bible. Use a good translation with scholarly notes.

**Other Texts:** For helpful background and handy reference we recommend:
Lawrence Boadt's *Reading the Old Testament* (cited as Boadt)
Eerdmans *Dictionary of the Bible* (cited as EDB)
Hammond's *Atlas of the Bible Lands* (cited as Hammond Atlas)

## Assignments

Each lesson is to be studied in preparation for your group discussion. For each biblical passage, study the biblical text and footnotes for that particular passage, complete the other assigned readings, and do the written work *on a separate page*.

I.1 INTRODUCTION TO WISDOM LITERATURE

I.2 THE BEAUTY OF WISDOM: PROVERBS 1–9

I.3 WISDOM IN CULTURAL CONTEXTS: PROVERBS 10, 16, 22–24, 28, 30–31

I.4 WISDOM CHALLENGED—GOD ON TRIAL: HABAKKUK; JOB 1–14, 42:7–17

I.5 WISDOM CHALLENGED—GOD ON TRIAL: JOB 19, 28–32, 36:22—42:17

I.6 THE FAILURE OF WISDOM: ECCLESIASTES (QOHELETH)

I.7 WISDOM REAFFIRMED: SIRACH (ECCLESIASTICUS) 1–4, 14–18, 20–23

I.8 WISDOM REAFFIRMED: SIRACH (ECCLESIASTICUS) 24–26, 30, 34, 38–39, 42–51

I.9 WISDOM REVISED: THE BOOK OF WISDOM (WISDOM OF SOLOMON)

I.10 UNIT ONE REVIEW

# I.1 Introduction to Wisdom Literature

**After studying this lesson, you will be able to:**

1. Identify the historical, literary, and social factors that contributed to the development of the wisdom traditions in the ancient Near East and in Israel.
2. Situate the Hebrew wisdom literature in the general theological tradition, in particular noting its foundation on the theme of creation rather than covenant.
3. Recognize the characteristics of wisdom literature.
4. Identify the influence of wisdom literature on the New Testament.

## Read

Boadt, pages 472–79; EDB article: "Wisdom, Wisdom Literature"; "The Historical Background for the Wisdom Writings: An Overview," #1 in the SUPPLEMENTARY READINGS at the back of this workbook

## Geography Task

Using the map on page 12 in your Hammond Atlas, review the locations of Egypt, Mesopotamia, and Israel.

## Important Terms

Creation, wisdom, wisdom literature

## Written Work

1. Wisdom writers base their claims not on revelations from God, as do the prophets, but on experience of the world around them. In what ways does your experience contribute to your understanding how God works in the world?

2. Wisdom writing, especially Proverbs, Job, and Ecclesiastes, seems to ignore the exodus, the Sinai Covenant, and the exile. Why do you think this is so?

3. Using the required readings for this week's lesson, identify the historical factors that contributed to the development of the wisdom traditions.

4. In light of the required readings for this week's lesson, what do you think are the three most interesting characteristics of wisdom literature?

5. Considering what you have learned from the readings for this week's lesson, how do you think Colossians 1:15–20 might have been influenced by wisdom literature?

## Exercise

(Note that this is part of the required study but does not always involve a written response.) As you work your way through the unit, choose a verse that you will memorize so that you are able to write it out with the proper citation (translation used and reference [book, chapter, and verse]). Suggestions are given for each lesson, but you may choose another verse that you like.

## ADDITIONAL SUGGESTIONS FOR THE STUDENT

**Memory Verse Suggestion**

For wisdom is a kindly spirit. (Wisdom 1:6a; NRSV)

**Further Reading**

*Catechism of the Catholic Church*, §216.

Camilla Burns, SNDdeN, "The Ways of Wisdom," *The Bible Today* 40, 6 (2002): 360–65.

James A. Fischer, *A Lighthearted View of Wisdom in the Bible: How to Read the Inspired Books* (New York/Mahwah, NJ: Paulist Press, 2002), 1–20.

Michael D. Guinan, OFM, "Images of God in the Wisdom Literature," *The Bible Today* 38, 4 (2000): 223–27.

Roland E. Murphy, *The Tree of Life: An Exploration of Biblical Wisdom Literature*, 3rd ed. (Grand Rapids, MI: Eerdmans, 2002), 1–15.

Irene Nowell, OSB, "Wisdom and the Word of God," *The Bible Today* 46, 5 (2008): 291–95.

***"Does the eagle soar at your command?"***
***Job 39:27***

*"Divine Scripture is the feast of wisdom, and the single books are the various dishes."*

—*St. Ambrose,* On the Duties of the Clergy, *1:165*

# I.2
# The Beauty of Wisdom: Proverbs 1–9

**After studying this lesson, you will be able to:**

1. Understand the literary form of proverbs, in particular the way that parallel construction works.
2. Identify characteristic concerns and themes that proverbs express and their function or use in the religious community.
3. Recognize the general outline of the Book of Proverbs, in particular the outline of Proverbs 1–9, and the major themes developed in these chapters.
4. Begin to recognize the links between the understanding of creation in Genesis 1 and in wisdom literature.

## Read

Proverbs 1–9; Boadt, pages 479–81; EDB article: "Proverb"; "Wisdom in Israel: Overview—Proverbs," #2 in the SUPPLEMENTARY READINGS at the back of this workbook

## Geography Task

Using the maps and charts on pages 10–11 in your Hammond Atlas, note the average monthly rainfall and temperature in Ancient Israel.

## Important Terms

Fear of the LORD, Lady Folly, Lady Wisdom, personification, proverb

## Written Work

1. a. According to Proverbs 1–2, what attitudes does the wisdom teacher expect from the pupil? Cite references.
   b. How are these attitudes significant for you as you seek wisdom?

2. According to Proverbs 3, what are the rewards for those who find wisdom and honor the LORD?

3. Personification is attributing human traits to inanimate or imaginary objects.
   a. How is folly personified in Proverbs 7 and 9?
   b. How is wisdom personified in Proverbs 8 and 9?
   c. How would you personify both folly and wisdom today?

4. In Proverbs 1–9, what evidence do you find to support the view that:
   a. wisdom is the gift of God? Cite references.
   b. wisdom is the result of human effort? Cite references.

5. a. According to Proverbs 3:19–20 and 8:22–31, what role does wisdom play in creation?
   b. Why do you think that the author of Proverbs in discussing creation includes a role for wisdom that is not found in Genesis?

6. Which proverb from this week's reading do you find most important for your understanding of your life? Explain.

## ADDITIONAL SUGGESTIONS FOR THE STUDENT

### Optional Challenges

1. Considering the role of women in ancient Israelite society, why do you think wisdom and folly would be personified as women?
2. Using Proverbs 2:16–19; 5:3–6; 6:20–29; and 7:5–27, discuss the theme of adultery and the way in which it reflects both the traditional secular wisdom of the ancient Near East and the religious wisdom of the Israelites.
3. In what ways might Proverbs 8 have influenced the theology of the prologue of John's gospel (John 1:1–18)? Consult EDB article "John, Gospel of: Theological Emphasis."

### Memory Verse Suggestion

The fear of the LORD is the beginning of wisdom, and the knowledge of the Holy One is insight. (Proverbs 9:10; NRSV)

### Further Reading

*Catechism of the Catholic Church*, §288 and §2465.

Anthony R. Ceresko, *Introduction to Old Testament Wisdom: A Spirituality for Liberation* (Maryknoll, NY: Orbis Books, 1999), 1–58.

James A. Fischer, *A Lighthearted View of Wisdom in the Bible: How to Read the Inspired Books* (New York/Mahwah, NJ: Paulist Press, 2002), 34–41.

Michael A. Machado, *The Book of Proverbs: The Wisdom of Words* (New York/Mahwah, NJ: Paulist Press, 2003).

Roland E. Murphy, *The Tree of Life: An Exploration of Biblical Wisdom Literature*, 3rd ed. (Grand Rapids, MI: Eerdmans, 2002), 15–19.

***"Refuse no kindness"—Proverbs 3:27***

# I.3 Wisdom in Cultural Contexts: Proverbs 10, 16, 22–24, 28, 30–31

**After studying this lesson, you will be able to:**

1. Situate Israelite wisdom literature in the broader context of wisdom reflections that were shared by many ancient Near Eastern peoples.
2. Identify both the practical and theological uses of proverbs in helping the people to live well.
3. Recognize in the Book of Proverbs the effects of parallel construction, in particular for emphasis, for contrast, and as an aid to memorization.
4. Recognize the diversity of themes and forms that characterize the Book of Proverbs.

## Read

Proverbs 10, 16, 22–24, 28, 30–31; EDB article: "Proverbs, Book of"; "Selections from the Instruction of Amen-em-Opet," #3 in the SUPPLEMENTARY READINGS at the back of this workbook

## Geography Task

Using the EDB article "Massa" and the map on page 12 in your Hammond Atlas, find the probable location of Massa.

## Important Term

Numerical proverb

## Written Work

1. Proverbs 10 has many guidelines for speaking. Choose two proverbs from chapter 10 that you find most helpful for your speaking. Explain why you chose each one.

2. a. Using Proverbs 16, what evidence do you find to support the view that nothing happens by human effort alone? Cite references.
   b. Using "Selections from the Instruction of Amen-em-Opet," #3 in the SUPPLEMENTARY READINGS at the back of this workbook, what evidence do you find to support the view that nothing happens by human effort alone? Cite references.
   c. Do you think Amen-em-Opet influenced the author of Proverbs? Why or why not?

3. Scholars believe that the "Words of the Wise" (Prov 22:17—24:22) have a special relationship with Amen-em-Opet. Using "Selections from the Instruction of Amen-em-Opet," #3 in the SUPPLEMENTARY READINGS at the back of this workbook, what evidence do you find to support this claim?

4. a. Using Proverbs 22–24, 28, choose *one* of the themes below and list the proverbs that apply to the theme you selected.
      - The teacher/student relationship
      - Family life
      - The benefits of wisdom for society
      - The attitude of the rich toward the poor

   b. Explain in greater detail two of the proverbs from your list to show what each contributes to the understanding of the theme you have chosen. Be specific.

5. Choose one of the numerical proverbs in Proverbs 30:15–31.
   a. Identify what links the items together in this proverb.
   b. Indicate how the observation of nature in this proverb helps you to understand the mysteries of your own life. Be specific.

6. Based on Proverbs 31:10–31, what characteristics does the ideal wife share with those who seek wisdom? Be specific.

## ADDITIONAL SUGGESTIONS FOR THE STUDENT

### Optional Challenges

1. Write at least two proverbs of your own, following the biblical form of parallel construction. Imitate the various types (e.g., "Better . . . , than . . ." a numerical proverb, a "blessed" saying, or the contrast of a wise person with a fool). Share these with your group.
2. Compose an original poem or prayer that illustrates one of the proverbs you have read.
3. In the style of Proverbs 31:10–31, write a portrait of the ideal husband who shares characteristics with wisdom.
4. What clues to the meaning of "fear of the LORD" (Prov 1:7) can you gather from the parallel constructions of Proverbs 1:7, 29; 2:5; 3:7; 8:13; 9:10; 10:27; 14:26–27; 15:16, 33; and 16:6?

### Memory Verse Suggestion

The human mind plans the way, but the LORD directs the steps. (Proverbs 16:9; NRSV)

### Further Reading

*Catechism of the Catholic Church*, §303, §1806, and §2219.

Anthony R. Ceresko, *Introduction to Old Testament Wisdom: A Spirituality for Liberation* (Maryknoll, NY: Orbis Books, 1999), 59–65.

James A. Fischer, *A Lighthearted View of Wisdom in the Bible: How to Read the Inspired Books* (New York/Mahwah, NJ: Paulist Press, 2002), 41–46.

Michael A. Machado, *The Book of Proverbs: The Wisdom of Words* (New York/Mahwah, NJ: Paulist Press, 2003).

Roland E. Murphy, *The Tree of Life: An Exploration of Biblical Wisdom Literature*, 3rd ed. (Grand Rapids, MI: Eerdmans, 2002), 19–32.

***"For a fool wisdom is an inaccessible fortress"***
***Proverbs 24:7***

# I.4 Wisdom Challenged—God on Trial: Habakkuk; Job 1–14, 42:7–17

**After studying this lesson, you will be able to:**

1. Identify the person and message of Habakkuk in their historical and social context.
2. Understand the structure, outline, literary style, and theological themes of the Book of Job, including elements of the traditional folk tale and the poetic dialogue.
3. Compare the theological issues in Job with wisdom themes and later Christian themes unavailable to the author of the Book of Job or the people of his time.

**Read**

Habakkuk; Job 1–14; 42:7–17; Boadt, pages 481–83; EDB articles: "Habakkuk, Book of," "Retribution," "Satan," and "Uz (place)"; "Wisdom in Israel: Overview—Habakkuk, Job," #2 in the SUPPLEMENTARY READINGS at the back of this workbook

**Geography Task**

Using EDB and the map on page 21 in your Hammond Atlas, locate the two most probable locations for Uz. Using the map on page 22 in your Hammond Atlas, locate the land of the Chaldeans.

**Important Terms**

Folktale, retribution, Satan

**Written Work**

1. The biblical tradition that Habakkuk inherited understood God as one who saves the chosen people.
   a. How does Habakkuk's current experience conflict with this tradition? Be specific.
   b. How does Habakkuk resolve this conflict? Be specific.

2. How might one of Habakkuk's woes (Hab 2:5–20) apply to our society today? Be specific.

3. How would you describe the relationship between God and Job that is found in the remnant of the traditional folktale (Job 1–2 and 42:7–17)?

4. Choose one of the speeches by Job's friends (Job 4–14). Indicate what the friend says about:
   a. why Job is suffering. Cite references.
   b. who God is. Cite references.
   c. how God acts. Cite references.

5. From your own experience, how would you answer Eliphaz's implicit claim that the guilty suffer and the innocent do not (Job 4:7–9)? Be specific.

6. Satan asks, "Does Job fear God for nothing?" (Job 1:9). Do you think humans serve God for themselves and for their own good, or is service of God with no expected rewards possible?

## ADDITIONAL SUGGESTIONS FOR THE STUDENT

**Optional Challenges**

1. Retell the story of Job as you would tell it to a child. Specify the age of the child.
2. Compare and contrast the skeptical questioning of God by Agur (Prov 30:1–9) with that of Habakkuk 1.

**Memory Verse Suggestions**

The righteous live by their faith. (Habakkuk 2:4b; NRSV)

"Naked I came from my mother's womb, and naked shall I return there; the LORD gave, and the LORD has taken away; blessed be the name of the LORD." (Job 1:21; NRSV)

**Further Reading**

*Catechism of the Catholic Church*, §2318.

Anthony R. Ceresko, *Introduction to Old Testament Wisdom: A Spirituality for Liberation* (Maryknoll, NY: Orbis Books, 1999), 66–78.

James A. Fischer, *A Lighthearted View of Wisdom in the Bible: How to Read the Inspired Books* (New York/Mahwah, NJ: Paulist Press, 2002), 47–62.

Harold S. Kushner, *When Bad Things Happen to Good People* (New York: Anchor, 2004; originally published in 1981).

Roland E. Murphy, *The Tree of Life: An Exploration of Biblical Wisdom Literature*, 3rd ed. (Grand Rapids, MI: Eerdmans, 2002), 33–37, 44–46.

Macrina Scott, OSF, *Bible Stories Revisited: Discover Your Story in the Old Testament* (Cincinnati, OH: St. Anthony Messenger Press, 1999), 253–64.

***"I shall stand at my post"—Habakkuk 2:1***

---

***About the Advice of Job's Neighbors***

*"Insofar as this doctrine is positive, it is sound and helpful... It contains much moral and religious truth but they spoil it by exaggeration. They are not willing to leave a margin of uncertainty, to admit limits to their understanding, to write after each of their theses 'If God so wills.' All the workings of divine providence must be clear to them, explicit, mathematical. They have fallen victims to the occupational hazard of the theologian: they forget that they are dealing with mystery. They have 'studied' God as a subject to be analyzed, predicted, and understood. And in forcing facts to agree with their understanding, they become wilfully dishonest (Job 13:6–11)."*

*—R. A. F. McKenzie, SJ, "Job," in* The New Jerome Biblical Commentary*, 30:5*

# I.5 Wisdom Challenged—God on Trial: Job 19, 28–32, 36:22—42:17

**After studying this lesson, you will be able to:**

1. Identify the structure and argument of the Book of Job.
2. Recognize the contributions of the Book of Job to probing the question of the mystery of suffering and God's role in it.
3. Recognize the major themes of the Book of Job and how they challenge a commonly accepted understanding of God and us.
4. Reflect more deeply on the ancient Israelite understanding of sin, suffering, and God's mysterious integration of power, justice, and mercy.
5. Appreciate the Book of Job for its powerful and sustained poetic reflection on the mystery of God and God's dealing with humanity.

**Read**

Job 19; 28–32; 36:22—42:17; EDB articles: "Behemoth," "Job, Book of," "Leviathan," and "Sheol"

**Geography Task**

Using your EDB, read "Naamathite," Shuah," and "Teman." Using your Hammond Atlas, locate possible locations for the homelands of Job's friends.

**Important Terms**

Redeemer/Vindicator (Go'el), Sheol

**Written Work**

1. In Job 19:25–27, Job experiences a moment of hope.
   a. What do you think these verses mean in the context of the Book of Job?
   b. What do you think these verses mean in the context of your life? Be specific.
2. What does the interlude in Job 28 contribute to your understanding of wisdom?
3. a. What kind of person does Elihu seem to be?
   b. What kind of God does Elihu describe?
4. Briefly describe the portrait of God implied in God's own words (Job 38–39).
5. How does Job's experience of the LORD contribute to your understanding of God?
6. Describe someone you know, or have heard of, whose situation is similar to Job's.

**Exercise**

Complete the "Self-Quiz: Mid-Unit One," #4 in the SUPPLEMENTARY READINGS at the back of this workbook.

## ADDITIONAL SUGGESTIONS FOR THE STUDENT

**Optional Challenges**

1. Depict Job's meeting with the LORD in an original picture, story, or poem.
2. Compare Job's experience of the LORD with Jeremiah's experience (Jer 12:1–6).
3. Draw an original picture of Behemoth and/or Leviathan.

**Memory Verse Suggestion**

For I know that my Redeemer lives, and that at the last he will stand upon the earth. (Job 19:25; NRSV; the composer Handel used this verse as the source for "I Know That My Redeemer Liveth" in his *Messiah*)

**Further Reading**

*Catechism of the Catholic Church*, §275 and §299.

Anthony R. Ceresko, *Introduction to Old Testament Wisdom: A Spirituality for Liberation* (Maryknoll, NY: Orbis Books, 1999), 79–90.

James A. Fischer, *A Lighthearted View of Wisdom in the Bible: How to Read the Inspired Books* (New York/Mahwah, NJ: Paulist Press, 2002), 47–62.

Harold S. Kushner, *When Bad Things Happen to Good People* (New York: Anchor, 2004; originally published in 1981).

Roland E. Murphy, *The Tree of Life: An Exploration of Biblical Wisdom Literature*, 3rd ed. (Grand Rapids, MI: Eerdmans, 2002), 37–48.

Macrina Scott, OSF, *Bible Stories Revisited: Discover Your Story in the Old Testament* (Cincinnati, OH: St. Anthony Messenger Press, 1999), 265–89.

***"Oh that my words were written down"***
***Job 19:23***

---

***Did You Know?***

*Job is one of the figures from the Bible whose experience and plight has often been explored by other literary artists. Examples include*

J. B., *a play by Archibald MacLeish*
*"Masque of Reason," a poem by Robert Frost*
God's Favorite, *a play by Neil Simon*

# I.6 The Failure of Wisdom: Ecclesiastes (Qoheleth)

**After studying this lesson, you will be able to:**

1. Recognize the historical, social, and theological background of the Book of Ecclesiastes (Qoheleth).
2. Identify the major themes of the Book of Ecclesiastes (Qoheleth), in particular the author's unique "this world" approach and his attitude toward wisdom and its value.
3. Compare the attitude of the author of the Book of Ecclesiastes (Qoheleth) to the hope expressed in other wisdom literature and also by New Testament authors.

## Read

Ecclesiastes (Qoheleth); Boadt, pages 483–85; EDB articles: "Ecclesiastes, Book of," "Megilloth," "Qoheleth," and "Vanity"; "Wisdom in Israel: Overview—Ecclesiastes (Qoheleth)," #2 in the SUPPLEMENTARY READINGS at the back of this workbook

## Important Terms

Megilloth, vanity

## Written Work

1. a. What does Ecclesiastes (Qoheleth) mean by the term *vanity*? (Use EDB and the Book of Ecclesiastes [Qoheleth].)
   b. Choose one of the items in Ecclesiastes (Qoheleth) 1–6 (wisdom, pleasure, toil, or wealth), and identify the reason why it is considered vanity. Be specific.
2. According to Ecclesiastes (Qoheleth) 3:1–15, what does the author think about who God is and why God acts? Be specific.
3. Do you agree with the statement in Ecclesiastes (Qoheleth) 3:12 that "there is nothing better for them [human beings] than to be happy and enjoy themselves as long as they live"? Why or why not?
4. According to Ecclesiastes (Qoheleth) 9:3–6, there is no afterlife. Would you behave any differently if you did not believe in a meaningful afterlife? Why or why not?
5. a. What does Ecclesiastes 11:7—12:8 have to say about the course of life?
   b. How well does this passage reflect your own experience? Explain.

*"Doubt is the key of knowledge."*

*—A Persian proverb*

## ADDITIONAL SUGGESTIONS FOR THE STUDENT

**Optional Challenges**

1. Do you agree with the Persian proverb, "Doubt is the key of knowledge"? Why or why not?
2. If you were a Jewish rabbi deciding whether to include Ecclesiastes (Qoheleth) in the canon, what arguments would you use for or against its inclusion?

**Memory Verse Suggestion**

For everything there is a season, and a time for every matter under heaven. (Ecclesiastes 3:1; NRSV)

**Further Reading**

*Catechism of the Catholic Church*, §1007.

Anthony R. Ceresko, *Introduction to Old Testament Wisdom: A Spirituality for Liberation* (Maryknoll, NY: Orbis Books, 1999), 91–114.

James A. Fischer, *A Lighthearted View of Wisdom in the Bible: How to Read the Inspired Books* (New York/Mahwah, NJ: Paulist Press, 2002), 63–74.

Roland E. Murphy, *The Tree of Life: An Exploration of Biblical Wisdom Literature*, 3rd ed. (Grand Rapids, MI: Eerdmans, 2002), 49–64.

Leo Plante, "Qoheleth: The Post-Modern Economist," *The Bible Today* 45, 6 (2007): 370–72.

***"Cast your bread upon water"—Ecclesiastes 11:1***

# I.7 Wisdom Reaffirmed: Sirach (Ecclesiasticus) 1–4, 14–18, 20–23

**After studying this lesson, you will be able to:**

1. Identify the social, historical, and religious situation of the Book of Sirach (Ecclesiasticus), in particular its place in the Israelite wisdom tradition.
2. Recognize the major themes and theological contributions of the Book of Sirach (Ecclesiasticus), in particular how the secular wisdom tradition is connected to the religious covenant tradition of Israel.
3. Appreciate the influence of Hellenistic culture on diaspora Jews and understand how the Book of Sirach (Ecclesiasticus) contributes to community awareness and identity.
4. Define the term *deuterocanonical* and explain why it is used with regard to books of the Catholic Bible.
5. Name the books that are identified as deuterocanonical.

## Read

Sirach (Ecclesiasticus) 1-4, 14-18, 20-23; Boadt, pages 486-87; EDB article: "Apocrypha"; "Wisdom in Israel: Overview–Sirach (Ecclesiasticus)," #2 and "Why Do Christians Have Different Bibles?" #5 in the SUPPLEMENTARY READINGS at the back of this workbook

## Geography Task

Using the map on page 26 in your Hammond Atlas, locate Alexandria, Egypt.

## Important Terms

Apocryphal, deuterocanonical, Septuagint

## Written Work

1. Imagine that you are speaking with a Protestant friend. Explain briefly how and why the Catholic canon differs from the Protestant canon.

2. In Sirach 2, what indications do you see that Sirach felt his readers' religious practice would be threatened by pressures around them? Cite references.

3. a. Choose one of the following themes. Compare and contrast the attitudes of Sirach and Ecclesiastes.
      i. Wealth (Sirach 14:3-19; Ecclesiastes 5:10—6:6 [5:9—6:6 NAB/NJB])
      ii. Wise and foolish (Sirach 20:1-31 [20:1-30 NAB]; 21:11-28; Ecclesiastes 2:12-17)
      iii. Search for wisdom (Sirach 14:20—15:10; Ecclesiastes 1:12-18; 7:11-12)
   b. Whose attitude do you prefer? Why?

4. The ancient Rabbi Simon the Just claimed that "the world is sustained by three things: by the law, by the temple service or worship, and by deeds of loving kindness." Choose either the theme of law or the theme of deeds of loving kindness and summarize what Sirach taught (Sir 1-4, 14-18, 20-23) about the importance of the theme that you chose. Cite references.

5. a. Quote three passages from Sirach that you think would be appropriate to ask children to memorize.
   b. At what age would you have them memorize each passage?
   c. For each of the passages, why did you choose this particular age?

6. a. Quote one wisdom saying in Sirach that you think still applies today. Why do you think it still applies?
   b. Quote one wisdom saying in Sirach that you think no longer applies today. Why do you think it no longer applies?

## ADDITIONAL SUGGESTIONS FOR THE STUDENT

### Optional Challenges

1. Write a conversation that might have occurred between Qoheleth and Sirach.
2. Sirach 3:19 is missing from most ancient manuscripts (see NRSV, NJB [NAB changes the versification]). Compose a verse that would fit as Sirach 3:19.
3. a. Compare and contrast God's punishment of sinners and their personal responsibility in Sirach 16:1–21 with that of Ezekiel 33:10–20 (see NRSV).
   b. How do these passages affect your attitudes about personal responsibility?

### Memory Verse Suggestion

Wisdom teaches her children and gives help to those who seek her. (Sirach 4:11; NRSV)

### Further Reading

*Catechism of the Catholic Church*, §1809, §2215, §2218, §2477, and §2536.

Anthony R. Ceresko, *Introduction to Old Testament Wisdom: A Spirituality for Liberation* (Maryknoll, NY: Orbis Books, 1999), 115–24.

James A. Fischer, *A Lighthearted View of Wisdom in the Bible: How to Read the Inspired Books* (New York/Mahwah, NJ: Paulist Press, 2002), 85–89.

Daniel J. Harrington, *Jesus Ben Sira of Jerusalem: A Biblical Guide to Living Wisely* (Collegeville, MN: Liturgical Press, 2005), 1–64.

Leslie Hoppe, OFM, "The Word of God in the Torah," *The Bible Today* 46, 5 (2008): 281–85.

Marjorie L. Kimbrough, *Stories Between the Testaments: Meeting the People of the Apocrypha* (Nashville, TN: Abingdon Press, 2000), 45–50.

Roland E. Murphy, *The Tree of Life: An Exploration of Biblical Wisdom Literature*, 3rd ed. (Grand Rapids, MI: Eerdmans, 2002), 65–72.

***"Throw stones at birds and you scare them away"***
***Sirach 22:20***

# I.8 Wisdom Reaffirmed: Sirach (Ecclesiasticus) 24–26, 30, 34, 38–39, 42–51

**After studying this lesson, you will be able to:**

1. Recall the historical, social, and religious context of the Book of Sirach (Ecclesiasticus) and how this context influences its meaning and message.
2. Evaluate the contribution of the Book of Sirach (Ecclesiasticus) to Jewish wisdom literature, in particular how the book unites teaching and worship, wisdom and Torah.

## Read

Sirach (Ecclesiasticus) 24–26, 30, 34, 38–39, 42–51; Boadt, pages 492–97; EDB articles: "Hellenism," and "Sirach, Wisdom of Jesus the Son of"

## Geography Task

Using the maps on pages 17 and 34 in your Hammond Atlas, locate Lebanon, Hermon, Engedi (Engaddi), and Jericho.

## Important Terms

Diaspora, Hellenism, Torah (Law)

## Written Work

1. In what ways does Sirach 24 show the unity of wisdom and Torah? Be specific.
2. What similarities and differences do you find between Sirach 24:3–12 and John 1:1–14? Cite references.
3. Evaluate Sirach's comments on women (Sir 25–26) in light of:
   a. his culture (e.g., Prov 31, Eccl 7:25–29)
   b. our culture today
4. What guidelines for living a genuine spiritual life (Sir 34) are most important for you? Why?
5. In light of what we know today, especially about human psychology, evaluate Sirach's advice on
   a. death and grief (Sir 38:16–23)
   b. rearing sons (Sir 30:1–13)
   c. rearing daughters (Sir 42:9–14)
6. Choose one ancestor from Sirach 44–50. Indicate how that ancestor acts as a model for Sirach's community to follow. Be specific.

## ADDITIONAL SUGGESTIONS FOR THE STUDENT

### Optional Challenges

1. Write original wisdom verses or a hymn in praise of wisdom in the style of Sirach 44–50 using contemporary persons.
2. How would you relate Sirach's recital of salvation history to that found in each of the following:
   a. Psalm 78
   b. Psalm 105
   c. Stephen's speech in Acts 7
3. According to Sirach 38–39, what should a wisdom teacher know? Cite references.
4. What does Sirach's prayer (Sir 36) reveal about his idea of God?

### Memory Verse Suggestion

A joyful heart is life itself, and rejoicing lengthens one's life span. (Sirach 30:22; NRSV)

### Further Reading

*Catechism of the Catholic Church*, §300, §696, §1809, and §2223.

EDB article: "Dispersion."

Anthony R. Ceresko, *Introduction to Old Testament Wisdom: A Spirituality for Liberation* (Maryknoll, NY: Orbis Books, 1999), 124–6.

James A. Fischer, *A Lighthearted View of Wisdom in the Bible: How to Read the Inspired Books* (New York/Mahwah, NJ: Paulist Press, 2002), 85–89.

Daniel J. Harrington, *Jesus Ben Sira of Jerusalem: A Biblical Guide to Living Wisely* (Collegeville, MN: Liturgical Press, 2005), 65–132.

Marjorie L. Kimbrough, *Stories Between the Testaments: Meeting the People of the Apocrypha* (Nashville, TN: Abingdon Press, 2000), 50–55.

Roland E. Murphy, *The Tree of Life: An Exploration of Biblical Wisdom Literature*, 3rd ed. (Grand Rapids, MI: Eerdmans, 2002), 72–81.

***"My child, when you are ill..."***
***Sirach 38:9***

---

*"The Bible is obviously not a book, or a set of books, intended to be read for entertainment with an admixture of insight and information... Rather, it wants to 'draw me out of myself,' using the medium of narrative to transform my sense of the world, urgently alert me to spiritual realities and moral imperatives I might have misconceived, or not conceived at all."*

*—Robert Alter, The World of Biblical Literature*

# I.9 Wisdom Revised: The Book of Wisdom (Wisdom of Solomon)

**After studying this lesson, you will be able to:**

1. Recognize the historical situation, structure, style, and message of the Book of Wisdom (Wisdom of Solomon).
2. Explain the meaning of attributed authorship for the Jews and other ancient Near Eastern peoples.
3. Note the Hellenistic influence on the Book of Wisdom (Wisdom of Solomon) and understand that this is a deuterocanonical work.
4. Identify the major themes and theological contributions of the Book of Wisdom (Wisdom of Solomon), in particular its revised understanding of wisdom and suggestion of immortality.

**Read**

Book of Wisdom (Wisdom of Solomon); Boadt, pages 488–91; EDB articles: "Soul" and "Wisdom of Solomon"; and "Wisdom in Israel: Overview—Book of Wisdom," #2 in the SUPPLEMENTARY READINGS at the back of this workbook

**Geography Task**

Using EDB and your Hammond Atlas, locate the general area of the Pentapolis, the Five Cities (Sodom, Gomorrah, Admah, Zeboiim, and Zoar) mentioned in Wisdom 10:6.

**Important Terms**

Immortality, midrash

**Written Work**

1. In Wisdom 1–2, what evidence do you find that:
   a. humans are made for eternal fellowship (immortality) with God? Cite references.
   b. God is not responsible for death? Cite references.

2. Wisdom 3:1–9 is the biblical text that seems to clearly change the Jewish understanding of the afterlife. It is often used at Christian funerals.
   a. How do you think this passage might comfort the bereaved at a funeral?
   b. How does this passage give you hope right now?

3. In Wisdom 3–4, how does the author of the Book of Wisdom use the belief in immortality to explain *one* of the following theological problems: suffering, childlessness, or early death?

4. In Solomon's speech (Wis 6:12—8:21):
   a. how is wisdom related to God? Cite references.
   b. what does wisdom do for humanity? Cite references.

5. a. What could be learned from Wisdom 11:23—12:2 about how God relates to the world?

b. Why do you think the liturgy of the Catholic Church reads this passage from the Book of Wisdom with the Zacchaeus story (Luke 19:1–10) on the Thirty-first Sunday of Ordinary Time, Cycle C?

6. a. The Book of Wisdom incorporates positive elements of the culture of its day to enhance an understanding of Jewish faith. Give at least one example of this from the Book of Wisdom.
   b. How might we today incorporate positive elements of our culture to enhance an understanding of Christian faith? Give at least one example.

## ADDITIONAL SUGGESTIONS FOR THE STUDENT

### Optional Challenges

1. Using Wisdom 7, explain wisdom's place and role:
   a. in creation
   b. in relation to humanity
2. Which passages from the Book of Wisdom are most helpful in your own search for wisdom? Why?

### Memory Verse Suggestion

But the souls of the righteous are in the hand of God, and no torment will ever touch them. (Wisdom 3:1; NRSV)

### Further Reading

*Catechism of the Catholic Church*, §41, §216, §269, §295, §299, §301, §302, §413, §1147, §1308, §1805–1809, and §2500.

EDB articles: "Afterlife, Afterdeath," and "Midrash."

Anthony R. Ceresko, *Introduction to Old Testament Wisdom: A Spirituality for Liberation* (Maryknoll, NY: Orbis Books, 1999), 139–85.

James A. Fischer, *A Lighthearted View of Wisdom in the Bible: How to Read the Inspired Books* (New York/Mahwah, NJ: Paulist Press, 2002), 89–93.

Marjorie L. Kimbrough, *Stories Between the Testaments: Meeting the People of the Apocrypha* (Nashville, TN: Abingdon, 2000), 39–45.

Michael Kolarcik, SJ, "The Wisdom of Solomon: Justice and Creation," *The Bible Today* 40, 6 (2002): 341–47.

Roland E. Murphy, *The Tree of Life: An Exploration of Biblical Wisdom Literature*, 3rd ed. (Grand Rapids, MI: Eerdmans, 2002), 83–96.

Irene Nowell, OSB, "Immortality in Wisdom," *The Bible Today* 40, 6 (2002): 354–59.

Gregory J. Polan, OSB, "Literary Creativity in the Wisdom of Solomon," *The Bible Today* 40, 6 (2002): 348–53.

***"Take a potter"—Wisdom 15:7***

# I.10
# Unit One Review

**You will be responsible for:**

1. A memory verse from the wisdom books studied in this unit, indicating the translation used and citing the reference.

2. The information in the following SUPPLEMENTARY READINGS at the back of this workbook:
   - #1 "The Historical Background for the Wisdom Writings: An Overview"
   - #2 "Wisdom in Israel: Overview"
   - #3 "Selections from the Instruction of Amen-em-Opet"
   - #4 "Self-Quiz: Mid-Unit One"
   - #5 "Why Do Christians Have Different Bibles?"

3. The location of the following places and areas on a map:
   Alexandria, Egypt, Israel, Jericho, Land of the Chaldeans, and Mesopotamia

**HELP JOB FIND A WAY OUT OF HIS DILEMMA!**

**GOD IS JUST [AND MUST REWARD GOOD AND PUNISH EVIL]**

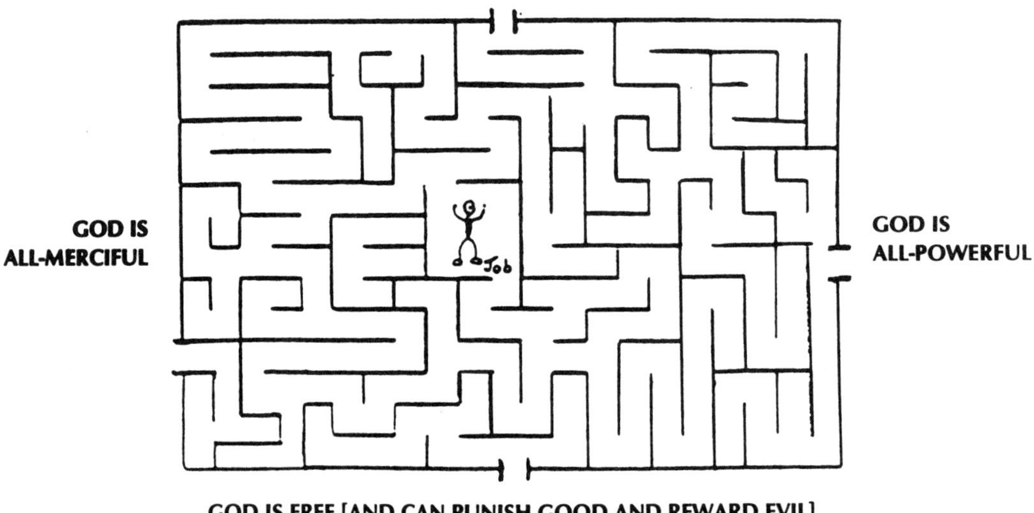


**GOD IS FREE [AND CAN PUNISH GOOD AND REWARD EVIL]**

# UNIT II
# Judaism in the Hellenistic World

**Objectives**

After completing this unit, you will be able to:

1. Explain the impact of Hellenistic culture and religion on diaspora Judaism.
2. Recognize didactic fiction as a literary form.
3. Identify Jewish apocalyptic literature.
4. Explain more fully the biblical canon and the deuterocanonical books.
5. Describe the Jewish feasts of Purim and Hanukkah.

## Textbooks

**Primary Text:** The Bible. Use a good translation with scholarly notes.

**Other Texts:** For helpful background and handy reference we recommend:
Lawrence Boadt's *Reading the Old Testament* (cited at Boadt)
Eerdmans *Dictionary of the Bible* (cited as EDB)
Hammond's *Atlas of the Bible Lands* (cited as Hammond Atlas)
Collegeville Commentary on Daniel

## Assignments

Each lesson is to be studied in preparation for your group discussion. For each biblical passage, study the biblical text and footnotes for that particular passage, complete the other assigned readings, and do the written work *on a separate page*.

II.1 JONAH

II.2 ESTHER

II.3 TOBIT

II.4 BARUCH

II.5 1 MACCABEES

II.6 2 MACCABEES

II.7 JUDITH

II.8 DANIEL 1–6, 13–14

II.9 DANIEL 7–12

II.10 UNIT TWO REVIEW

# II.1 Jonah

**After studying this lesson, you will be able to:**

1. Identify the historical setting, structure, and literary style of the Book of Jonah.
2. Recognize that the message of scripture comes in a variety of literary forms and need not be reduced to historical fact to be true or important.
3. Recognize the meaning and importance of the literary genre of didactic fiction for the Jewish community.
4. Identify the major themes and theological contributions of the Book of Jonah.

## Read

The Book of Jonah; Boadt, pages 466–71; EDB article: "Jonah, Book of"; "Truth and Its Many Expressions," #6, and "Judaism in the Hellenistic World: Overview—Jonah," #7 in the SUPPLEMENTARY READINGS at the back of this workbook

## Geography Task

Using the map on page 22 in your Hammond Atlas, locate Nineveh. Read the EDB article, "Tarshish (Place)."

## Important Terms

Didactic fiction, literary form/genre

## Written Work

1. Conversion is a key theme of the Book of Jonah. Who is converted? Describe the conversion of each.

2. If you rewrote the Jonah story today, who would you name in place of the Ninevites? Why?

3. Irony is a major literary device in this story.
   a. Give an example of irony that you find in the story.
   b. What point is the author making by using irony in this example?

4. When in your own life did/do you "escape to Tarshish" instead of "going to Nineveh"?

5. Read Luke 11:29–32 and Matthew 12:40–42.
   a. What does Luke illustrate by using Jonah?
   b. What does Matthew add?

## Exercise

As you work your way through the unit, choose a verse that you will memorize so that you are able to write it out with the proper citation (translation used and reference [book, chapter, and verse]). Suggestions are given for each lesson, but you may choose another that you like.

## ADDITIONAL SUGGESTIONS FOR THE STUDENT

**Optional Challenges**

1. Present the Book of Jonah in an original poem, play, or picture.
2. Research the story of Jonah as depicted in ancient Christian art. Present your findings to your group.
3. Write a sermon based on the Book of Jonah for Christians involved in ministry.

**Memory Verse Suggestion**

I called to the LORD out of my distress, and he answered me; out of the belly of Sheol I cried, and you heard my voice. (Jonah 2:2; NRSV; see Jonah 2:3 NAB, NJB)

**Further Reading**

*Catechism of the Catholic Church*, §1431 and §1432.

John F. Craghan, "The Book of Jonah and the Challenge to Forgive," *The Bible Today* 45, 2 (2007): 80–84.

James A. Fischer, *A Lighthearted View of Wisdom in the Bible: How to Read the Inspired Books* (Mahwah, NJ: Paulist Press, 2002), 75–83.

Timothy A. Lenchak, SVD, "God in the Book of Jonah," *The Bible Today* 38, 4 (2000): 206–10.

Joseph F. Wimmer, OSA, "Jonah's Lessons on Conversion," *The Bible Today* 43, 6 (2005): 377–81.

***"Jonah prayed"—Jonah 2:2***

---

*"What do we find in these books? Ideas, yes. Stories, yes. Words, naturally. But now we know after studying that they contain an unknown world full of mystery, wonder, and courage. We [Jews] chose language over violence, history over geography, time over space, imagination over reality. Away from Jerusalem we lived in Jerusalem. In exile we found the way to worship in the Temple. How did we do it? We closed our eyes, and we let the past dominate the present through the words we read in the Book of Moses, and then we taught them. Unlike other traditions and civilizations, Judaism is not a heritage offered by the dead to the living: it is a heritage offered by the living to the living."*

*—Elie Wiesel, foreword to* Torah With Love, *by David Epstein and Suzanne Stutman*

# II.2 Esther

**After studying this lesson, you will be able to:**

1. Identify the historical, cultural, and religious situation for which the Book of Esther was written, as well as its structure and literary style.
2. Recognize the author's intention to use the story of Esther and Mordecai as didactic fiction (a teaching device).
3. Describe the major themes and theological contributions of the Hebrew and Greek versions of the Book of Esther.
4. Recognize that the Greek additions to the Book of Esther are deuterocanonical.
5. Describe the Jewish feast of Purim and its relationship to the story of Esther.

## Read

The Book of Esther; Boadt, pages 497–99; EDB articles: "Esther, Book of," "Esther, Additions to," "Purim," and "Persia"; "Judaism in the Hellenistic World: Overview—Esther," #7 in the SUPPLEMENTARY READINGS at the back of this workbook

## Geography Task

Using the maps on pages 22, 23, and 24 in your Hammond Atlas, identify the two areas into which the Persian Empire extends beyond the borders of the Assyrian or Babylonian Empires.

## Important Term

Purim

## Written Work

1. Summarize three things you learned about the Persian Empire from your reading of EDB and Boadt.

2. a. Read the Hebrew version of the Book of Esther (without the Greek additions). What do you think is the meaning of the story?
   b. Read the Book of Esther again, this time including the Greek additions. How do the Greek additions change the meaning of the story?
   c. Which version of the story do you prefer? Why?

3. A key theme of Esther is reversal. For example, Queen Vashti was humbled and the humble Esther became queen. Identify at least three other examples of reversal.

4. a. What similarities do you find between the story of Joseph (Gen 37–45) and the story of Esther? Cite references.
   b. Why do you think the author of the Hebrew version of Esther reflects themes from the story of Joseph?

5. Choose either the prayer of Esther or that of Mordecai. What can you learn from that prayer for your personal prayer? Be specific.

6. Research the feast of Purim by consulting a Jewish friend, books, or the Internet. Summarize your findings and cite your sources.

## ADDITIONAL SUGGESTIONS FOR THE STUDENT

**Optional Challenges**

1. Choose one of the characters in the Book of Esther. Explain how she or he might have been a role model for diaspora Jews.
2. The hostility between Mordecai, who is of the family of Saul (A:1), and Haman, who is of the family of Agag, king of the Amalekites (A:17), is better understood by studying the relationship between their ancestors.
   a. What can you find in 1 Samuel that throws light on the Book of Esther? Cite references.
   b. What meaning do you find in the Jewish actions in Esther 9:10 and 9:15?

**Memory Verse Suggestion**

But save us by your hand, and help me, who am alone and have no helper but you, O Lord. (Esther 14:14; NRSV Greek version; see NAB Esther C:14b; NJB 4:17b)

**Further Reading**

*Catechism of the Catholic Church*, §269.

Marjorie L. Kimbrough, *Stories Between the Testaments: Meeting the People of the Apocrypha* (Nashville, TN: Abingdon, 2000), 33–38.

***"So he set the royal diadem"—Esther 2:17***

---

*"Remember the Book of Esther which we read twice a year on Purim? God's name is not mentioned once in that book. Not once. And the Talmud is wondering why? The answer, I believe, is at the end of the book where we are told that Jews, for a day or two, became avengers. God, I believe, says, 'If this is so, my place is not here.'"*

*—Elie Wiesel*

# II.3 Tobit

**After studying this lesson, you will be able to:**

1. Identify the historical, cultural, and religious situation for which the Book of Tobit was written.
2. Recognize the author's intention to use the Tobit story as didactic fiction (a teaching device).
3. Discuss the literary structure, major themes, and theological contributions of the Book of Tobit.
4. Discover the post-exilic theological ideas presented in the Book of Tobit (e.g., angels).
5. Recognize the Book of Tobit as deuterocanonical.

## Read

The Book of Tobit; Boadt, pages 501–2; EDB articles: "Angel," "Blindness," "Burial," "Raphael," and "Tobit, Book of"; "Judaism in the Hellenistic World: Overview—Tobit," #7 in the SUPPLEMENTARY READINGS at the back of this workbook

## Geography Task

Using the map on page 24 of your Hammond Atlas, locate Ecbatana in Media.

## Important Term

Angels

## Written Work

1. a. What historical event is referred to in Tobit 1:18 (see 2 Kings 19:35–37)?
   b. Why is it significant that the story makes reference to this historical event?

2. Family life is an important theme in the Book of Tobit.
   a. List three virtues or virtuous acts that encourage the family. Cite references.
   b. How might these be of value in strengthening the family today?

3. Prayer is an important theme in the Book of Tobit.
   a. How does each of the prayers in this book begin?
   b. What do the prayers help you to understand about your relationship with God?

4. a. From the Book of Tobit, what do you learn about angels? Cite references.
   b. How is this description of an angel as presented in the Book of Tobit similar to and/or different from your understanding of angels?
   c. Describe a time in your life when you encountered an "angel" from God.

5. a. What similarities do you find between the Book of Tobit and the infancy narrative in Luke's gospel?
   b. Do you think Luke had the Book of Tobit in mind when he composed his infancy narrative? Why or why not?

6. Describe some person or situation you have heard about that is similar to a character or situation in the Book of Tobit.

## ADDITIONAL SUGGESTIONS FOR THE STUDENT

**Optional Challenges**

1. Compose an original poem or picture based on Tobit.
2. a. What similarities do you find between Revelation 21 and Tobit 13? Be specific.
   b. Do you think Revelation 21 was influenced by Tobit 13? Why or why not?
3. What kind of journey have you been on where you have encountered a "big fish"? What sense can you make of Raphael's advice to "hold on" and "not let go"?

**Memory Verse Suggestion**

Blessed are you because you have made me glad. It has not turned out as I expected, but you have dealt with us according to your great mercy. (Tobit 8:16; NRSV)

**Further Reading**

*Catechism of the Catholic Church*, §336, §2300, §2361, and §2447.

Alexander A. DiLella, OFM, "Health and Healing in Tobit," *The Bible Today* 37, 2 (1999): 69–73.

Daniel J. Harrington, SJ, "Prayers in Tobit," *The Bible Today* 37, 2 (1999): 86–90.

Marjorie L. Kimbrough, *Stories Between the Testaments: Meeting the People of the Apocrypha* (Nashville, TN: Abingdon, 2000), 11–22.

Amy-Jill Levine, "Women in Tobit," *The Bible Today* 37, 2 (1999): 80–85.

Irene Nowell, OSB, "Aging in the Book of Tobit," *The Bible Today* 37, 2 (1999): 74–79.

Macrina Scott, OSF, *Bible Stories Revisited: Discover Your Story in the Old Testament* (Cincinnati, OH: St. Anthony Messenger Press, 1999), 239–51.

*"Catch the fish"—Tobit 6:4*

# II.4
# Baruch

**After studying this lesson, you will be able to:**

1. Identify the structure, literary style, and theological themes of the Book of Baruch.
2. Recognize the historical, social, and religious situations reflected in the Book of Baruch.
3. Recognize the Book of Baruch as deuterocanonical.
4. Recognize Baruch 6 as the Letter of Jeremiah to the Babylonian exiles.

**Read**

The Book of Baruch; Boadt, pages 502–3; EDB articles: "Baruch, Book of," and "Chaldea"; "Judaism in the Hellenistic World: Overview—Baruch," #7 and "Canon Quiz," #8 in the SUPPLEMENTARY READINGS at the back of this workbook

**Geography Task**

On the map on page 22 of your Hammond Atlas, locate Babylonia and the land of Chaldea.

**Important Term**

Pseudonymous authorship

**Written Work**

1. Describe the religious practices and attitudes of post-exilic Judaism as reflected in the Book of Baruch. Cite references.

2. Baruch 3:9–15, 3:32—4:4 is used at the Easter Vigil. Why do you think the church proclaims this reading at that liturgy? Be specific.

3. The most frequent refrain in Baruch 6 is: "They are not gods; do not be afraid of them." How might this refrain help you in your efforts to live a Christian life? Be specific.

4. Select a passage from Baruch that you would consider suitable for use on some occasion. Indicate the occasion for which you would use it, and explain your choice.

5. a. What important theological or other insights do you find in Baruch?
   b. Do you think it would matter if Baruch were not in the Bible?

6. Define each term as it is used by Catholics:
   a. canon of scripture
   b. Septuagint
   c. deuterocanonical books
   d. apocrypha

**Exercises**

1. Memorize the names of the seven deuterocanonical books.
2. Check your familiarity with the deuterocanonical books by taking the "Canon Quiz," #8 in the SUPPLEMENTARY READINGS at the back of this workbook.

## ADDITIONAL SUGGESTIONS FOR THE STUDENT

**Optional Challenges**

1. Using Tobit and Baruch, describe the attitude of diaspora Jews toward Jerusalem.
2. Illustrate a passage from Baruch with an original drawing.
3. Identify the characters mentioned in Baruch 1 and show how they are related to each other and to the beginnings of the exile.
4. Where else in scripture besides Baruch 1:11 is there mention of prayer for pagan rulers? What is the content of these prayers? Cite references.

**Memory Verse Suggestion**

Hear the commandments of life, O Israel; give ear, and learn wisdom! (Baruch 3:9; NRSV)

**Further Reading**

*Catechism of the Catholic Church*, §2112.

Marjorie L. Kimbrough, *Stories Between the Testaments: Meeting the People of the Apocrypha* (Nashville, TN: Abingdon, 2000), 57–60.

***"When women do the offering to these gods"***
***Baruch 6:29***

---

*"For no question can be solved by means of another which itself waits solution; nor, in the opinion of those possessed of sense, can an ambiguity be explained by means of another ambiguity, or enigmas by means of another greater enigma, but things of such character receive their solution from those which are manifest, and consistent, and clear."*

—*Irenaeus,* Against Heresies, *2.10.1*

# II.5
# 1 Maccabees

**After studying this lesson, you will be able to:**

1. Identify the general historical and social situation in Palestine from the time of Alexander the Great (d. 323 BC) to the time of Antiochus IV and the Maccabean revolt (ca. 168 BC).
2. Recognize the structure, literary style, intended audience, and characteristic themes of 1 Maccabees.
3. Recognize 1 Maccabees as deuterocanonical.

**Read**

1 Maccabees 1–9; Boadt, pages 503–6; EDB articles: "Alexander, #1," "Antiochus," "Hasmonean," "Maccabees," "Maccabees, First and Second Books of, 'Historical Background,' '1 Maccabees,'" "Ptolemy," and "Seleucid"; "Judaism in the Hellenistic World: Overview—1 Maccabees," #7 and "Who's Who in Maccabees," #9 in the SUPPLEMENTARY READINGS at the back of this workbook

**Geography Task**

Using the index and the maps in your Hammond Atlas, trace the events of 1 Maccabees 5.

**Important Terms**

Hasmonean, Maccabees, Ptolemy, Seleucid

**Written Work**

1. Using your EDB, write a paragraph indicating some reasons why Alexander is called "the Great."

2. Farewell discourses are a common literary form in scripture. These are words spoken by a great leader to his children or followers just before death.
   a. Identify three examples in the Bible of such farewell discourses and read one of them.
   b. What similarities do you find between the farewell discourse you chose and the farewell discourse of Mattathias (1 Macc 2:49–69)?

3. Give three examples of how the Maccabean revolt was inspired by memories of the Israelites' national history. Cite references.

4. a. How would you characterize Jewish attitudes toward Hellenism? Cite references.
   b. If you were living in the time of the Maccabees, what would be your attitude toward Hellenism? Why?

5. a. Do you think the Maccabees' use of violence was justified? Why or why not?
   b. Do you believe any wars are just? Why or why not?

## ADDITIONAL SUGGESTIONS FOR THE STUDENT

**Optional Challenge**

Imagine you are a Roman senator who has heard the Jewish envoys (1 Macc 8:19–22). Why would you want to enter into an alliance with the Jews? Be specific.

**Memory Verse Suggestion**

And so observe, from generation to generation, that none of those who put their trust in him will lack strength. (1 Macc 2:61; NRSV)

**Further Reading**

*Catechism of the Catholic Church*, §2306–2317.
Marjorie L. Kimbrough, *Stories Between the Testaments: Meeting the People of the Apocrypha* (Nashville, TN: Abingdon, 2000), 75–87.

---

*"Of all the questions raised by these books [Maccabees] perhaps the most fundamental is the relation between religion and politics. Other questions, such as theodicy, or the justice of the power that rules the world, arise in the context of this fundamental problem. The reason that the justice of God is temporarily in doubt is that the political order is disrupted. The religion persecuted by Antiochus was very specifically the religion of the Jews. What was at issue was not only their cultic worship, but their very identity as a distinct people with a distinctive way of life. The question of theodicy appears in this context as the question of the vindication of the Jewish way of life in a hostile world."*

—*John J. Collins,* Old Testament Message Commentaries, *volume 15*

***"Judas sent them to Rome"—1 Maccabees 8:17***

# II.6
# 2 Maccabees

**After studying this lesson, you will be able to:**

1. Recall the particular historical and social situation in Palestine during the time of the Maccabean revolt and the importance of the struggle for independence.
2. Recognize the structure, literary style, intended audience, and theological themes of 2 Maccabees.
3. Recognize that 2 Maccabees is deuterocanonical.
4. Explain the meaning of the feast of Hanukkah.
5. Identify elements of Catholic theology that have roots in 2 Maccabees.

## Read

2 Maccabees 1–7, 9–10, 12:38–46, 15; EDB articles: "Dedication, Feast of," "Maccabees, First and Second Books of, '2 Maccabees,'" "Midrash," and "Resurrection, 'Intertestamental Literature'"; "Judaism in the Hellenistic World: Overview—2 Maccabees," #7 in the SUPPLEMENTARY READINGS at the back of this workbook

## Geography Task

Using the map on pages 25 and 29 of your Hammond Atlas, locate Idumea, Beth-zur, Joppa, Jamnia, Modein, Gilead, and Carnaim.

## Important Terms

Hanukkah (Chanukah), intercessory prayer (of the "saints"), prayer for the dead, resurrection

## Written Work

1. a. Which passages give you an insight into the editor (epitomist/abridger) of 2 Maccabees?
   b. How would you summarize his attitude toward his task of abridging the five-volume work of Jason of Cyrene?

2. Imagine that you are a Jewish parent trying to explain Hanukkah in a way that will make it meaningful for your child today. What would you say? Be specific.

3. a. Explain the similarities and differences between Mattathias and Eleazar.
   b. Which do you think is more important in the church, warriors (like the Maccabees) or martyrs (like Eleazar)? Why?

4. a. What is the teaching of 2 Maccabees about life after death? Cite references.
   b. Why do you think the author of 2 Maccabees professes this particular belief in life after death?

5. How might Catholic doctrine be different if we did not have 2 Maccabees? Be specific.

## Exercises

Complete the Self-Quiz: Mid-Unit Two, #10 in the SUPPLEMENTARY READINGS at the back of this workbook.

## ADDITIONAL SUGGESTIONS FOR THE STUDENT

**Optional Challenges**

1. Create an original picture, poem, or prayer based on 2 Maccabees.
2. How has the practice of prayer for the dead in 2 Maccabees 12:46 had an important role in development of the church's tradition? For further information, see the *Catechism of the Catholic Church*, §§1030–1032.
3. Research the feast of Hanukkah by consulting a Jewish friend, books, or a reliable source on the Internet. Summarize your findings and cite your sources.

**Memory Verse Suggestion**

I do not know how you came into being in my womb. It was not I who gave you life and breath, nor I who set in order the elements within each of you. Therefore the Creator of the world, who shaped the beginning of humankind and devised the origin of all things, will in his mercy give life and breath back to you again, since you now forget yourselves for the sake of his laws. (2 Maccabees 7:22–23; NRSV)

**Further Reading**

*Catechism of the Catholic Church*, §297, §363, §992, and §§1030–1032.

Marjorie L. Kimbrough, *Stories Between the Testaments: Meeting the People of the Apocrypha* (Nashville, TN: Abingdon, 2000), 89–98.

***"Nehemiah founded a library"***
***2 Maccabees 2:13***

---

***Did You Know?***

- *Mary Renault's novel,* Funeral Games: The Combat of Alexander's Heirs, *gives a vivid picture of the breakup of Alexander the Great's empire after his death and provides background on the period of the Maccabees.*
- *Henry Wadsworth Longfellow wrote a poetic drama entitled* Judas Maccabeus.
- *Handel composed oratorios on Judas Maccabeus and Esther.*
- *Racine, the great French dramatist, wrote a play entitled* Judith, *based on the Book of Judith.*
- *Over 150 plays about Judith were written in the Middle Ages!*

# II.7 Judith

**After studying this lesson, you will be able to:**

1. Identify the historical, cultural, and religious situation of the Book of Judith.
2. Recognize the author's intention to use the Judith story as didactic fiction (a teaching device).
3. Discuss the literary structure, major themes, and theological contributions of the Book of Judith.
4. Recognize that the Book of Judith is deuterocanonical.

**Read**

The Book of Judith; Boadt, pages 499–500; EDB article: "Judith, Book of"; "Judaism in the Hellenistic World: Overview—Judith," #7 in the SUPPLEMENTARY READINGS at the back of this workbook

**Geography Task**

On the map on page 23 of your Hammond Atlas, locate the places mentioned in Judith 1:1.

**Important Term**

Widow

**Written Work**

1. It has been said that the Book of Judith has so many exodus themes that it may have been written for the Passover celebration. What evidence do you find to support this claim? Cite references.

2. a. Compare and contrast Judith and Esther regarding:
      i. their personalities.
      ii. the way they deal with pagan authorities.
   b. If you could choose to be one of these women, which one would you choose and why?

3. a. Identify the character traits of Uzziah in this story. Cite references.
   b. How might he represent a type that still exists today? Be specific.

4. What advice would you imagine Judith giving to women of today?

5. There are many allusions to Old Testament stories in the Book of Judith.
   a. Name at least three.
   b. Why do you think the author makes so many Old Testament allusions?

6. In its liturgy, the Catholic Church uses Judith 13:18a, 19–20, and 15:9–10 in regard to the Blessed Virgin Mary. Why do you think the church applies these texts to Mary?

## ADDITIONAL SUGGESTIONS FOR THE STUDENT

**Optional Challenges**

1. Do further research on Hellenism and write a brief account of it, in particular its relationship to scripture.
2. The Book of Judith is thought to have been written in the time of the Maccabees. What reflections of these times do you find in the Book of Judith? Be specific.

**Memory Verse Suggestion**

You are the glory of Jerusalem, you are the great boast of Israel, you are the great pride of our nation! (Judith 15:9; NRSV)

**Further Reading**

*Catechism of the Catholic Church*, §489 and §2585.

Marjorie L. Kimbrough, *Stories Between the Testaments: Meeting the People of the Apocrypha* (Nashville, TN: Abingdon, 2000), 23–31.

Irene Nowell, OSB, "Seven Gifts of the Deuterocanonical Books," *The Bible Today* 45, 3 (2007): 143–47.

Macrina Scott, OSF, *Bible Stories Revisited: Discover Your Story in the Old Testament* (Cincinnati, OH: St. Anthony Messenger Press, 1999), 227–38.

*"Led the women as they danced"—Judith 15:13*

# II.8 Daniel 1–6, 13–14

**After studying this lesson, you will be able to:**

1. Identify the structure, literary style, intended audience, and historical and social situation of the Book of Daniel.
2. Recognize the characteristic themes and theological contributions of the Book of Daniel, especially its influence on New Testament authors.
3. Note that the Greek additions to the Book of Daniel are deuterocanonical.

## Read

Daniel 1–6, 13–14; Boadt, pages 506–15; Collegeville Commentary on Daniel 1–6, 13–14; EDB articles: "Daniel, #4," "Daniel, Additions to," and "Daniel, Book of"; "Judaism in the Hellenistic World: Overview—Daniel," #7 in the SUPPLEMENTARY READINGS at the back of this workbook

## Geography Task

Using page 23 in your Hammond Atlas, note the city of Babylon and the extent of the Babylonian Empire.

## Important Terms

Fiery furnace, handwriting on the wall, lion's den

## Written Work

1. a. Choose Daniel 2, 4, or 5. Compare the story in the chapter you have chosen with that in Genesis 41. What similarities or connections do you notice? Cite references.
   b. Why do you think the author of Daniel made these connections? Be specific.

2. Choose Daniel 2, 3, 4, 5, or 6. What does the story teach that you think is still applicable today about:
   a. God? Be specific.
   b. humanity? Be specific.

3. Daniel 1–6 and 13–14 present stories about Daniel as a hero.
   a. What heroes do you have in your life?
   b. Why do you consider them heroes?

4. What differences do you notice between Daniel 13 and the other stories in Daniel?

5. Most stories in Daniel show believers confronted with choices about their loyalty to God. How do you find yourself challenged with choices about your loyalty to God? Be specific.

6. The deuterocanonical prayer of Azariah and the three young men (Dan 3:24–90; NRSV addition) is frequently used in the Liturgy of the Hours. How might this prayer enhance your own prayer life?

## ADDITIONAL SUGGESTIONS FOR THE STUDENT

### Optional Challenges

1. a. Rewrite a story from Daniel 1–6 so that it will be suitable for a child of a certain age.
   b. Tell the story to a child of this age, make note of the child's reaction, and discuss this reaction with your group.
2. Compose an original story like one of those in the Book of Daniel for a modern setting.
3. Write an original poem, prayer, or meditation based upon Daniel 4.
4. Draw an original picture of some scene from Daniel.
5. a. Describe anti-Jewish feelings shown in Esther and Daniel. Cite references.
   b. Where do you find anti-Jewish feelings in today's world? Be specific.

### Memory Verse Suggestion

To you, O God of my ancestors, I give thanks and praise, for you have given me wisdom and power, and have now revealed to me what we asked of you, for you have revealed to us what the king ordered. (Daniel 2:23; NRSV)

### Further Reading

*Catechism of the Catholic Church*, §2112 and §2416.

Marjorie L. Kimbrough, *Stories Between the Testaments: Meeting the People of the Apocrypha* (Nashville, TN: Abingdon, 2000), 65–74.

***"But the angel of the Lord came down"—Daniel 3:49***

# II.9
# Daniel 7–12

**After studying this lesson, you will be able to:**

1. Identify the characteristic themes and theological contribution of the apocalyptic sections of the Book of Daniel, in particular their importance and use by Christian authors.
2. Recognize the use of the apocalyptic genre to give encouragement to Jews during the Maccabean revolt.
3. Recognize the Book of Daniel as a blending of the genres of didactic fiction and apocalyptic.

## Read

Daniel 7–12; Collegeville Commentary on Daniel 7–12; EDB articles: "Gabriel" and "Michael, #11"

## Geography Task

Using page 22 in your Hammond Atlas, locate the city of Susa in the province of Elam.

## Important Terms

Apocalyptic genre, apocalyptic literature

## Written Work

1. In the vision of Daniel 7, what do you think the author intends to represent by:
   a. the sea?
   b. the four beasts?
   c. the ten horns?
   d. the little horn?
   e. the Ancient One?
   f. the son of man/human being?

2. a. If you were a Jew suffering under the persecution of Antiochus IV Epiphanes, what hopeful message would you find for your life in Daniel 7? Be specific.
   b. What message does Daniel 7 have for Christians today?

3. In Daniel 8, what do you think the author intends to represent by:
   a. the ram?
   b. the goat?
   c. the great horn on the goat?
   d. the little horn on the goat?
   e. the beautiful land?
   f. the sanctuary of the prince of the host?

4. In Daniel 9,
   a. what passages of Jeremiah is Daniel trying to interpret? Cite references.
   b. how does Gabriel interpret the seventy years? Cite references.

5. Describe the teaching of Daniel on the resurrection. Cite references.

6. What do you find in Daniel 7–12 that might be helpful for your own spiritual life?

## ADDITIONAL SUGGESTIONS FOR THE STUDENT

### Optional Challenges

1. Compose an original vision like one of Daniel's, teaching the same theological message but using events of modern history.
2. a. Summarize what you have learned about Antiochus Epiphanes from the books of 1 and 2 Maccabees, Judith, and Daniel. Cite references.
   b. Identify additional things you can learn by reading "Antiochus" in your EDB.

### Memory Verse Suggestion

Many of those who sleep in the dust of the earth shall awake, some to everlasting life, and some to shame and everlasting contempt. (Daniel 12:2; NRSV)

### Further Reading

*Catechism of the Catholic Church*, §330, §440, §664, §992, and §998.

Lawrence Boadt, CSP, "Appreciating the Book of Daniel," *The Bible Today* 42, 6 (2004): 336–41.

Catherine Cory, "Beastly Kings and the Heavenly Messiah," *The Bible Today* 42, 6 (2004): 349–54.

Daniel J. Harrington, SJ, "The Greatest Story Never Told: Reading the Bible with a Visual Imagination," *The Bible Today* 46, 1 (2008): 21–26.

Dorothy Jonaitis, OP, *Unmasking Apocalyptic Texts: A Guide to Preaching and Teaching* (New York/Mahwah, NJ: Paulist Press, 2005), 91–100.

Paul Niskanen, "Kingdoms, Dominions, and the Reign of God," *The Bible Today* 42, 6 (2004): 342–48.

***"At that time Michael will arise"***
***Daniel 12:1***

# II.10
# Unit Two Review

**You will be responsible for:**

1. A memory verse from the books studied in this unit, indicating the translation used and citing the reference.

2. The information in the following SUPPLEMENTARY READINGS at the back of this workbook:
   #7 "Judaism in the Hellenistic World: Overview"
   #8 "Canon Quiz"
   #10 "Self-Quiz: Mid-Unit Two"

3. The location of Nineveh on a map.

4. Identifying the historical background and describing the theological meaning of the Jewish feasts of Purim and Hanukkah in light of the books studied in this unit.

5. Defining *Hellenism* and describing some major ways in which it influenced Judaism during the three hundred years prior to the birth of Jesus.

6. Identifying all the deuterocanonical books and parts of books.

7. Identifying the terms:
   a. canonical
   b. deuterocanonical
   c. apocryphal
   d. Septuagint (Greek canon)
   e. Masoretic text (Hebrew canon)

**Exercises to assist your study**

1. If the deuterocanonical books we have studied in this unit were removed from the Bible, what three things do you think would be the greatest losses?
2. Give three examples from the books we have studied in this unit of ways in which they help you to understand the New Testament.

*"I was sent to you to test you."*

*(Tobit 12:14a; NRSV)*

# UNIT III
# Early Christian Development

**Objectives**

After completing this unit, you will be able to:

1. Identify the chronology, geography, and socio-cultural environment of Christianity in the last third of the first century.
2. Explain the message proclaimed by Matthew in his gospel.
3. Use the methods and skills of narrative, historical, literary, and redaction criticism in studying the Gospel of Matthew.
4. Explain the message of the Pastoral and Catholic letters of the New Testament.
5. Apply the messages of the biblical books studied in this unit to the contemporary world.

## Textbooks

**Primary Text:** The Bible. Use a good translation with scholarly notes.

**Other Texts:** For helpful background and handy reference we recommend:
Joseph F. Kelly, *An Introduction to the New Testament for Catholics* (cited as Kelly)
Kurt Aland, ed., *Synopsis of the Four Gospels*
George Montague, *Companion God* (cited as Montague)
Eerdmans *Dictionary of the Bible* (cited as EDB)
Hammond's *Atlas of the Bible Lands* (cited as Hammond Atlas)

## Assignments

Each lesson is to be studied in preparation for your group discussion. For each biblical passage, study the biblical text and footnotes for that particular passage, complete the other assigned readings, and do the written work *on a separate page.*

III.1 MATTHEW 1–4

III.2 MATTHEW 5–7

III.3 MATTHEW 8–10

III.4 MATTHEW 11–17

III.5 MATTHEW 18–23

III.6 MATTHEW 24–28

III.7 NEW TESTAMENT LETTERS I: 1 and 2 TIMOTHY, TITUS, JAMES

III.8 NEW TESTAMENT LETTERS II: 1 and 2 PETER, JUDE

III.9 HEBREWS

III.10 UNIT THREE REVIEW

# III.1 Matthew 1–4

**After studying this lesson, you will be able to:**

1. Recall the gospel genre, the theological perspective of each evangelist, and skills of critical reading and interpretation.
2. Identify the narrative structure, sources, date, authorship, probable location, and community situation of Matthew's gospel.
3. Begin recognizing the literary style, theological emphases, and guiding principles of Matthew's editorial work (redaction) vis-à-vis his source materials: Mark's gospel, *Q*, and Matthew's own special community materials, *M*.
4. Explain the importance of Matthew's infancy narrative in the light of his entire gospel.

**Read**

Matthew 1–4; Montague, pages 1–47; EDB articles: "Matthew, Gospel according to" and "Genealogy"; "The Three Stages of the Composition of the Gospels (Vatican II)," #11, "The Synoptic Gospels and Their Sources," #12, "Material Usually Allotted to *Q*," #13, "*M* Passages," #14, and "The Gospel of Matthew: Overview," #15," in the SUPPLEMENTARY READINGS at the back of this workbook

**Geography Task**

On the map provided in "Jesus' Journey in Matthew," #16 in the SUPPLEMENTARY READINGS at the back of this workbook, trace Jesus' activities and journeys in Matthew 1–4. You will note that a number of events take place in unnamed locations. As you trace, focus on the named locations and the general areas and directions of the journey. You might want to use different colored pencils for each lesson.

**Important Terms**

Emmanuel, fulfillment texts, infancy narrative, *M* passages, *quelle* (*Q*), son of God, synoptic problem

**Written Work**

1. In Matthew 1:
   a. List the titles Matthew applies to Jesus. Cite references.
   b. What clue does each give about the identity and mission of Jesus?

2. In Matthew 1–2, the infancy narratives, identify two ways in which Matthew expresses:
   a. continuity with the Jewish tradition
   b. openness to the Gentile world

3. Locate the first words that Jesus speaks in Matthew's gospel. What hints do they contain about Jesus' identity and mission?

4. Choose one of the fulfillment quotes (introduced by "This was to fulfill…" or similar wording) that Matthew uses in his gospel (Matt 1–4).
   a. What is the original context of this Old Testament passage (i.e., what did the text mean when it was first written)?
   b. What connection do you think Matthew sees between the Old Testament passage and the life of Jesus?

5. Locate Matthew 4:1–11, the temptation of Jesus, in your *Synopsis of the Four Gospels*.
   a. What significant changes does Matthew make to Mark's version? Cite references.
   b. How do the changes help you to understand the meaning of this event for Matthew?
   c. Why do you think Matthew's order is different from the order in Luke? Be specific.

6. Which passage from Matthew 1–4 was most meaningful to you? Why?

**Exercises**

1. Mountains play an important role in the Gospel of Matthew. As you read the gospel, note the mention and the name of any mountain, and what happens on it. Think about how Matthew is using geography to express his theology.
2. As you work your way through the unit, choose a verse that you will memorize so that you are able to write it out with the proper citation (translation used and reference [book, chapter, verse]). Suggestions are given for each lesson, but you may want to choose another verse.

## ADDITIONAL SUGGESTIONS FOR THE STUDENT

**Optional Challenges**

1. How would you explain to a friend why Matthew's gospel has an infancy narrative and Mark's does not?
2. Summarize briefly the theological message of Matthew's infancy narrative.
3. Find the first words of Jesus in Mark and Luke. In what ways do they contribute to the evangelist's distinctive portrait of Jesus' identity and mission in that gospel?

**Memory Verse Suggestion**

"Look, the virgin shall conceive and bear a son, and they shall name him Emmanuel," which means, "God is with us." (Matthew 1:23; NRSV)

**Further Reading**

*Catechism of the Catholic Church*, §430, §439, §486, §497, §528, §530, §535, §1223, §1224, and §2666.

Raymond Brown, *Introduction to the New Testament* (New York: Doubleday, 1998), 171–78, 203–22.

Joseph A. Grassi, "Matthew's Gospel of Justice," *The Bible Today* 38, 4 (2000): 234–38.

Joseph F. Kelly, *An Introduction to the New Testament for Catholics* (Collegeville, MN: Liturgical Press, 2006), 113–19.

John P. Meier, *Matthew* (Collegeville, MN: Liturgical Press, 1980), 1–36.

Thanh Van Nguyen, SVD, "In Solidarity with Strangers: The Flight into Egypt," *The Bible Today* 45, 4 (2007): 219–24.

Mary Margaret Pazdan, "Jesus is Baptized in the Jordan," *The Bible Today* 44, 3 (2006): 137–43.

Daniel J. Scholz, *Jesus in the Gospels and Acts: Introducing the New Testament* (Winona, MN: Saint Mary's Press, 2009), 74–89.

***The Magi come—Matthew 2:9***

# III.2
# Matthew 5–7

**After studying this lesson, you will be able to:**

1. Identify the structure and theological themes developed in the first major discourse of Matthew, the Sermon on the Mount.
2. Describe the nature of beatitude as used by Matthew.
3. Make connections with the Old Testament, especially with the role of Torah in Judaism, with Jewish religious practices, and with the wisdom traditions that guided post-exilic Jews.

## Read

Matthew 5–7; Montague, pages 47–106; EDB articles: "Beatitudes" and "Sermon on the Mount/Plain"

## Geography Task

Note that the Sermon on the Mount takes place on an unnamed mountain in Galilee.

## Important Terms

Antithesis, beatitude, discourse, kingdom of God

## Written Work

1. Using the beatitudes (Matt 5:1–12), answer the following questions:
   a. What does the first part of a beatitude describe?
   b. What does the second part describe?
   c. What values in our society do the beatitudes most challenge? Explain.

2. Locate Matthew 5:1–12 and Luke 6:17–26 in your *Synopsis of the Four Gospels*.
   a. To what audience does Jesus direct his words in Matthew and in Luke?
   b. What might the location (Matthew's mount, Luke's plain) reveal about each evangelist's theology?
   c. How do Luke's beatitudes differ from Matthew's?
   d. Why do you think Luke and Matthew have different beatitudes?

3. Matthean Themes: Continuity with the Old Testament
   Choose one of the six antitheses in Matthew 5:21–46.
   a. To what Old Testament teaching does this text refer?
   b. Is Jesus' teaching more or less demanding than the tradition? Why?
   c. How has Jesus' teaching influenced your life?

4. Choose one of the three religious practices in Matthew 6:1–18. Then explain:
   a. What is to be avoided?
   b. What is to be done?
   c. What rewards can be expected for doing this?

5. Redacting with Matthew:
   *In order to appreciate Matthew's creative shaping of his sources, you will have a chance each week to try your hand at working a quotation into Matthew's gospel text. Make any editorial changes you find necessary. Remember, you are not really changing the inspired text. There are no right or wrong answers. This is an imaginative exercise. Its goal is to help you appreciate how Matthew worked with his sources as you make the editorial decisions to insert the quote.*

Suppose that upon completing his gospel, Matthew read Luke's Acts of the Apostles and liked the saying of Jesus that "It is more blessed to give than to receive" (Acts 20:35).

a. If you were Matthew, where would you include this saying in the Sermon on the Mount? Write out the saying in its context (including the verses before and after) as you want it to read so that it fits smoothly into the gospel text. You may need to make additional editorial changes, depending on where you choose to insert the saying.
b. Explain the reason for your choice of location.

6. Which passage from Matthew 5–7 is most meaningful to you? Why?

## ADDITIONAL SUGGESTIONS FOR THE STUDENT

### Optional Challenges

1. Using Jesus' message about anxiety in Matthew 6:25–34, what would you say in order to calm a worried friend?
2. In what ways does Jesus' teaching style resemble that of a teacher in the Jewish wisdom tradition? Be specific.
3. In the style of Matthew's Sermon on the Mount, how do you think Jesus would complete the following saying "You have heard it said, 'Remember to keep holy the Sabbath,' but I say to you __________"? Explain why you completed the saying in that way.

### Memory Verse Suggestion

For where your treasure is, there your heart will be also. (Matthew 6:21; NRSV)

### Further Reading

*Catechism of the Catholic Church*, §1716–§1724, §1965–§1972, §2518–§2519, and §2759–§2856.

EDB articles: "Divorce," "Kingdom of God, Kingdom of Heaven: 'New Testament,'" "Righteousness."

Raymond Brown, *Introduction to the New Testament* (New York: Doubleday, 1998), 178–80.

Joseph F. Kelly, *An Introduction to the New Testament for Catholics* (Collegeville, MN: Liturgical Press, 2006), 119–21.

Frank J. Matera, "Jesus and the Law: Matthew's View," *The Bible Today* 39, 5 (2001): 271–76.

John P. Meier, *Matthew* (Collegeville, MN: Liturgical Press, 1980), 37–76.

Michael O'Connor, "Scripture and Its Fulfillment," *The Bible Today* 41, 3 (2003): 154–59.

Gregory J. Polan, OSB, "Psalm 2: The Reign of God and His Anointed One," *The Bible Today* 44, 6 (2006): 337–42.

Daniel J. Scholz, *Jesus in the Gospels and Acts: Introducing the New Testament* (Winona, MN: Saint Mary's Press, 2009), 89–90.

***"Knock and the door will be opened"—Matthew 7:17***

# III.3 Matthew 8–10

**After studying this lesson, you will be able to:**

1. Recognize the meaning and purpose of the miracles of Jesus and the role they play in relation to the kingdom of God in Matthew's gospel.
2. Describe Matthew's understanding of the demands of Christian discipleship.
3. Identify the structure and theological emphases of the second major discourse, the missionary discourse (Matt 10).

## Read

Matthew 8–10; Montague, pages 107–34; EDB articles: "Apostle" and "Disciple"

## Geography Task

On the map provided in "Jesus' Journey in Matthew," #16 in the SUPPLEMENTARY READINGS at the back of this workbook, trace Jesus' activities and journeys in Matthew 8–10. You will note that a number of events take place in unnamed locations. As you trace, focus on the named locations and the general areas and directions of the journey. You might want to use different colored pencils for each lesson.

## Important Terms

Apostle, disciple, miracle, mission

## Written Work

1. Choose one of the miracles in Matthew 8–9. For the miracle you chose:
   a. What, if anything, indicates the seriousness of the situation? Cite a reference.
   b. How is the miracle performed? Cite a reference.
   c. What, if any, is the response of those present? Cite a reference.
   d. What, if any, is the role of faith and prayer in the miracle?

2. a. Summarize the demands of discipleship in Matthew 8:18–22 and 9:9–13.
   b. What do you think these teachings might reveal about the situation of Matthew's community? Be specific.
   c. How might these teachings apply to your life? Explain.

3. Locate Matthew 9:18–26 in your *Synopsis of the Four Gospels*:
   a. What significant changes does Matthew make to Mark's text?
   b. How do Matthew's changes reveal his emphasis on who Jesus is?

4. Matthean Theme: Sharing in Jesus' Mission
   Using Matthew 10, the missionary discourse, answer the following questions:
   a. How does the mission of the disciples reflect that of Jesus (see Matthew 4:23; 9:35 for a summary of the mission of Jesus)? Be specific.
   b. How does the mission of the disciples continue to be lived in the church today? Give examples.

5. Redacting with Matthew:
   *In order to appreciate Matthew's creative shaping of his sources, you will have a chance each week to try your hand at working a quotation into Matthew's gospel text. Make any editorial changes you find*

*necessary. Remember, you are not really changing the inspired text. There are no right or wrong answers. This is an imaginative exercise. Its goal is to help you appreciate how Matthew worked with his sources as you make the editorial decisions to insert the quote.*

Suppose that upon completing his gospel, Matthew wanted to use the saying of Jesus reported by Clement of Alexandria [*Stromateis*, 1.24.158], "Ask for the great things and God will add to you what is small."

a. If you were Matthew, where would you include this saying in Matthew 8–10? Write out the saying in its context (including the verses before and after) as you want it to read so that it fits smoothly into the gospel text. You may need to make additional editorial changes, depending on where you choose to insert the saying.
b. Explain the reason for your choice of location.

## ADDITIONAL SUGGESTIONS FOR THE STUDENT

### Optional Challenges

1. A friend reads Matthew 10 and wonders if being a disciple of Jesus means rejecting family duties. What would you say?
2. What guidelines can you find in Matthew 4–10 for distinguishing genuine disciples from false ones? Cite references.
3. How would you explain to a puzzled friend the paradox in Matthew 10:39 about saving and losing one's life?

### Memory Verse Suggestion

The centurion said, "Lord, I am not worthy to have you come under my roof; but only speak the word, and my servant will be healed." (Matthew 8:8; NRSV)

### Further Reading

*Catechism of the Catholic Church*, §1386, §1505, §1509, §1816, §2100, §2145, §2232, and §2610.

Barbara E. Bowe, RSCJ, "'Sharper than any Two-Edged Sword': The Word of God in the Synoptic Gospels," *The Bible Today* 46, 5 (2008): 301–5.

Raymond Brown, *Introduction to the New Testament* (New York: Doubleday, 1998), 180–83.

Joseph F. Kelly, *An Introduction to the New Testament for Catholics* (Collegeville, MN: Liturgical Press, 2006), 121–23.

John P. Meier, *Matthew* (Collegeville, MN: Liturgical Press, 1980), 79–115.

***Cure of the woman with a hemorrhage***
***Matthew 9:20–22***

# III.4 Matthew 11–17

**After studying this lesson, you will be able to:**

1. Recognize the nature and purpose of parables in Matthew's gospel.
2. Identify the structure and theological emphases in the gospel's third major discourse (Matt 13).
3. Recognize Matthew's use of Peter to exemplify both the positive (rock) and the negative (stumbling block) possibilities of Christian discipleship.
4. Recognize Matthew's understanding of who Jesus is and what it means to be his disciple.

## Read

Matthew 11–17; Montague, pages 135–94; EDB articles: "Peter" and "Transfiguration"

## Geography Task

On the map provided in "Jesus' Journey in Matthew," #16 in the SUPPLEMENTARY READINGS at the back of this workbook, trace Jesus' activities and journeys in Matthew 11–17. You will note that a number of events take place in unnamed locations. As you trace, focus on the named locations and the general areas and directions of the journey. You might want to use different colored pencils for each lesson.

## Important Terms

Parable, primacy of Peter

## Written Work

1. In Matthew 11–12:
   a. List the titles used to describe Jesus. Cite references.
   b. What does each title reveal about the identity and mission of Jesus?

2. a. What do Matthew's unique parables of the treasure and the pearl (Matt 13:44–46) reveal about the kingdom of God?
   b. How do these parables challenge you?

3. a. Summarize the message of the parables of the weeds (Matt 13:24–30) and the net (Matt 13:47–50).
   b. What do you think this message might reveal about the situation of Matthew's community?
   c. How might this message apply to your life? Explain.

4. Matthean Themes: Peter
   Locate Matthew 14:22–33 in your *Synopsis of the Four Gospels.*
   a. What significant changes does Matthew make to Mark's text? Cite references.
   b. How do Matthew's changes reveal his emphasis on the person of Peter?

5. Redacting with Matthew:
   *In order to appreciate Matthew's creative shaping of his sources, you will have a chance each week to try your hand at working a quotation into Matthew's gospel text. Make any editorial changes you find necessary. Remember, you are not really changing the inspired text. There are no right or wrong answers. This is an imaginative exercise. Its goal is to help you appreciate how Matthew worked with his sources as you make the editorial decisions to insert the quote.*

Suppose that upon completing his gospel, Matthew wanted to use the saying of Jesus reported by Origen [Homily 20, 3 *on Jeremiah*], "He who is near me is near the fire; he who is far from me is far from the kingdom."

a. If you were Matthew, where would you include this saying in Matthew 11–17? Write out the saying in its context (including the verses before and after) as you want it to read so that it fits smoothly into the gospel text. You may need to make additional editorial changes, depending on where you choose to insert the saying.
b. Give the reason for your choice of location.

6. Which passage from Matthew 11–17 is most meaningful to you? Why?

## ADDITIONAL SUGGESTIONS FOR THE STUDENT

### Optional Challenges

1. What would you tell a friend who asked you: "Why did Jesus teach about the kingdom of God with parables and not plainly so we can understand?"
2. Write a parable about the kingdom of heaven in the style of Matthew using imagery taken from life today.
3. How might Matthew 13:51–52 be a self-portrait of Matthew the evangelist? Be specific.
4. Research the use of Matthew 16 on the role of Peter and its importance for the church's understanding of the role of the papacy (See EDB, "Peter" and the *Catechism of the Catholic Church*).

### Memory Verse Suggestion

Come to me, all you that are weary and are carrying heavy burdens, and I will give you rest. (Matthew 11:28; NRSV)

### Further Reading

*Catechism of the Catholic Church*, §153, §240, §424, §439 §440, §448, §540, §546, §550, §552–§555, §579, §581, §586, §590, §719, §765, §787, §827, §881, §1335, §1444, §1583, §1864, §2517, §2603, and §2701.

EDB articles: "Parables" and "Pharisees."

Raymond Brown, *Introduction to the New Testament* (New York: Doubleday, 1998), 183–91.

Raymond Brown et al., *Peter in the New Testament: A Collaborative Assessment by Protestant and Roman Catholic Scholars* (Reprint; Eugene, OR: Wipf & Stock Publishers, 2002).

Demetrius R. Dumm, OSB, "The Transfiguration of Jesus," *The Bible Today* 44, 3 (2006): 157–62.

Joseph F. Kelly, *An Introduction to the New Testament for Catholics* (Collegeville, MN: Liturgical Press, 2006), 123–26.

John P. Meier, *Matthew* (Collegeville, MN: Liturgical Press, 1980), 119–98.

Irene Nowell, OSB, "Peter in the Gospels of Mark and Matthew," *The Bible Today* 43, 4 (2005): 216–21.

Pheme Perkins, *Peter: Apostle for the Whole Church (Personalities of the New Testament)* (Minneapolis, MN: Augsburg Fortress Publishers, 2000).

Barbara E. Reid, OP, "Puzzling Passages: Matthew 13:24–30, 36–43," *The Bible Today* 41, 4 (2003): 259–60.

Daniel J. Scholz, *Jesus in the Gospels and Acts: Introducing the New Testament* (Winona, MN: Saint Mary's Press, 2009), 90–94.

# III.5 Matthew 18–23

**After studying this lesson, you will be able to:**

1. Identify the structure and theological emphases of Matthew 18–23, in particular Matthew's fourth major discourse (Matt 18).
2. Note how Matthew's narrative style heightens the tension between Jesus and the Jewish authorities in the second half of his gospel.
3. Apply Matthew's theology of church to the twenty-first century church.

## Read

Matthew 18–23; Montague, pages 195–260; EDB articles: "Church" and "Binding and Loosing"

## Geography Task

On the map provided in "Jesus' Journey in Matthew," #16 in the SUPPLEMENTARY READINGS at the back of this workbook, trace Jesus' activities and journeys in Matthew 18–23. You will note that a number of events take place in unnamed locations. As you trace, focus on the named locations and the general areas and directions of the journey. You might want to use different colored pencils for each lesson.

## Important Terms

Authority, bind and loose, church

## Written Work

1. In Matthew 18:1–14:
   a. Who are the "little ones" (Matt 18:6, 10, and 14)?
   b. How are these "little ones" to be treated?
   c. What does the example of the child reveal about the meaning of discipleship that can apply to your own life? Be specific.

2. In Matthew 16:18–19 and 18:17–18, Matthew uses the word for church (Greek *ekklesia*) to describe the Christian community.
   a. In each of these passages who has the power to bind and loose?
   b. What does this reveal about Matthew's understanding of the church?
   c. Do you think the steps that Matthew outlines (Matt 18:15–18) would work today? Why or why not?
   d. How does Peter's question and Jesus' response (Matt 18:21–22), including the parable about forgiveness (Matt 18:23–35), inform your understanding of binding and loosing?

3. Matthean Themes: Fulfillment
   Locate Matthew 21:1–9 in your *Synopsis of the Four Gospels*.
   a. What significant changes does Matthew make to Mark's text?
   b. What do Matthew's changes reveal about his understanding of Jesus?

4. In what ways does Matthew 21–23 show a heightening tension between Jesus and the Jewish authorities? Cite at least two examples.

5. Redacting with Matthew:
   *In order to appreciate Matthew's creative shaping of his sources, you will have a chance each week to try your hand at working a quotation into Matthew's gospel text. Make any editorial changes you find necessary. Remember, you are not really changing the inspired text. There are no right or wrong answers. This is an imaginative exercise. Its goal is to help you appreciate how Matthew worked with his sources as you make the editorial decisions to insert the quote.*

Suppose that upon completing his gospel, Matthew wanted to use the saying of Jesus reported by Tertullian [*On Baptism*, xx, 2]: "No one can attain the kingdom of heaven who has not gone through temptation."

a. If you were Matthew, where would you include this saying in Matthew 18–23? Write out the saying in its context (including the verses before and after) as you want it to read so that it fits smoothly into the gospel text. You may need to make additional editorial changes, depending on where you choose to insert the saying.
b. Give the reason for your choice of location.

6. Which passage from Matthew 18–23 is most meaningful to you? Why?

**Exercise**

Complete "Self-Quiz: Mid-Unit Three," #17 in the SUPPLEMENTARY READINGS at the back of this workbook.

## ADDITIONAL SUGGESTIONS FOR THE STUDENT

### Optional Challenges

1. How would you explain to a rich friend Jesus' saying: "It is easier for a camel to pass through a needle's eye than for a rich person to enter the kingdom of God" (Matt 19:23–24)?
2. In Matthew 20:1–16, the parable of the laborers, what do you learn about God and about admission to God's kingdom?
3. Suppose that upon completing his gospel, Matthew wanted to use the saying of Jesus reported in the apocryphal Gospel of Thomas, #60: "They saw a Samaritan carrying a lamb; he was going to Judea. Jesus said to His disciples, 'Why does he carry the lamb?' They said to Him, 'That he may kill it and eat it.' He said to them, 'As long as it is alive he will not eat it, but only when he has killed it and it has become a corpse.' They said, 'Otherwise he cannot do it.' He said to them, 'You yourselves seek a place for yourselves in repose, lest you become a corpse and be eaten.'"
   a. *If you were Matthew,* where would you include this saying in Matthew 18–23? Write out the saying in its context (including the verses before and after) as you want it to read so that it fits smoothly into the gospel text. You may need to make additional editorial changes so that the saying fits smoothly in the gospel text, depending on where you choose to insert it.
   b. Give the reason for your choice of location.

### Memory Verse Suggestion

Whoever becomes humble like this child is the greatest in the kingdom of heaven. (Matthew 18:4; NRSV)

### Further Reading

*Catechism of the Catholic Church*, §439, §447, §526, §546, §575, §581, §605, §755, §796, §982, §1444, §1610, §1614, §1615, §1620, §2052, §2053, §2111, §2227, §2285, §2364, §2384, §2472, and §2785.

Raymond Brown, *Introduction to the New Testament* (New York: Doubleday, 1998), 191–98.

Dennis Hamm, SJ, "Matthew's Portrait of the Disciples," *The Bible Today* 42, 5 (2004): 287–91.

Daniel J. Harrington, SJ, "The Wisdom of Jesus," *The Bible Today* 42, 5 (2004): 274–79.

Joseph F. Kelly, *An Introduction to the New Testament for Catholics* (Collegeville, MN: Liturgical Press, 2006), 126–29.

John P. Meier, *Matthew* (Collegeville, MN: Liturgical Press, 1980), 199–275.

# III.6 Matthew 24–28

**After studying this lesson, you will be able to:**

1. Identify the structure and theological themes of Matthew's fifth major discourse, the apocalyptic discourse (Matt 24–25).
2. Identify the structure and theological emphases in Matthew's passion narrative and resurrection account, and how they compare with other gospel accounts.
3. Recognize how Matthew's gospel responds to the needs of his community, in particular its idea of who Jesus is, what it means to be a Christian disciple, and how community members ought to relate to their former Jewish neighbors and to the other Christian communities that make up the whole Christian Church.
4. Distinguish Matthew's unique contributions to Christology, ecclesiology, eschatology, and understanding of discipleship.

## Read

Matthew 24–28; Montague, pages 287–364; "Four Ways to Follow Jesus," #18, "*Nostra Aetate* §4, #19, and "The Jewish People and Their Sacred Scripture in the Christian Bible," #20 in the SUPPLEMENTARY READINGS at the back of this workbook

## Geography Task

Using the map on page 35 of your Hammond Atlas, trace Jesus' movements during the events of Holy Week. Using the map provided in "Jesus' Journey in Matthew," #16 in the SUPPLEMENTARY READINGS at the back of this workbook, trace the movements of the resurrected Jesus in Matthew 28. You might want to use different colored pencils for each lesson.

## Important Terms

Great commission, judgment (of the nations)

## Written Work

1. Matthean Themes: Doing Rather than Saying
   In Matthew 25:31–46, many who seem not to know the Lord are saved whereas many who claim to recognize the Lord are not.
   a. According to the parable, on what is salvation or condemnation based?
   b. How does this parable compare to your own notion about the basis of salvation?

2. a. With reference to SUPPLEMENTARY READING #20, how does Matthew's passion account (Matt 26–27) shift blame for Jesus' death from the Romans to the Jewish people?
   b. Why do you think Matthew wrote his account that way?
   c. How would you explain this account to a Jewish friend?

3. Locate Matthew 27:45–54 in your *Synopsis of the Four Gospels*.
   a. Compare and contrast Matthew 27:45–54 with *one* other gospel account.
   b. What do you think makes these similarities and differences significant?

4. Why do you think that Matthew introduces and stresses the presence and the role of the guards in his account of the burial and resurrection of Jesus (Matt 27:57—28:15)?

5. a. Having concluded your study of Matthew's gospel, summarize your own reflections about Matthew's presentation of who Jesus is.
   b. Summarize your own reflections about what it means to be a Christian disciple.
   c. Which aspects of Matthew's gospel do you find most helpful?
   d. Which aspects of Matthew's gospel do you find most challenging for your life today?

**Exercise** Review "The Events of Holy Week (According to the Synoptic Gospels)" on page 37 of your Hammond Atlas.

## ADDITIONAL SUGGESTIONS FOR THE STUDENT

**Optional Challenge** Write an editorial about the death of Jesus for *one* of these papers and make sure you follow the editorial perspective of that newspaper:

a. *The Sanhedrin Sentinel*
b. *The Roman Reporter*
c. *The Voice of the Jewish People*

**Memory Verse Suggestion** And Jesus came and said to them, "All authority in heaven and on earth has been given to me. Go therefore and make disciples of all nations, baptizing them in the name of the Father and of the Son and of the Holy Spirit, and teaching them to obey everything that I have commanded you. And remember, I am with you always, to the end of the age." (Matthew 28:18–20; NRSV)

**Further Reading**

*Catechism of the Catholic Church*, §2, §80, §189, §232, §585, §578, §579, §591, §640, §691, §767, §849, §857, §1122, §1373, §1444, §1936, §2443–§2449, §2831, and §2849.

EDB articles: "Commission, Great," "Eschatology: Jesus and the Gospels," "Lord's Supper: Matthew and Mark," "Passion Narratives," and "Resurrection: New Testament."

Raymond Brown, *Introduction to the New Testament* (New York: Doubleday, 1998), 198–203.

Joseph F. Kelly, *An Introduction to the New Testament for Catholics* (Collegeville, MN: Liturgical Press, 2006), 129–35.

John P. Meier, *Matthew* (Collegeville, MN: Liturgical Press, 1980), 277–374.

Marianne Race, CSJ, "Galilee's Influence on Jesus," *The Bible Today* 41, 2 (2003): 72–79.

Daniel J. Scholz, *Jesus in the Gospels and Acts: Introducing the New Testament* (Winona, MN: Saint Mary's Press, 2009), 94–98.

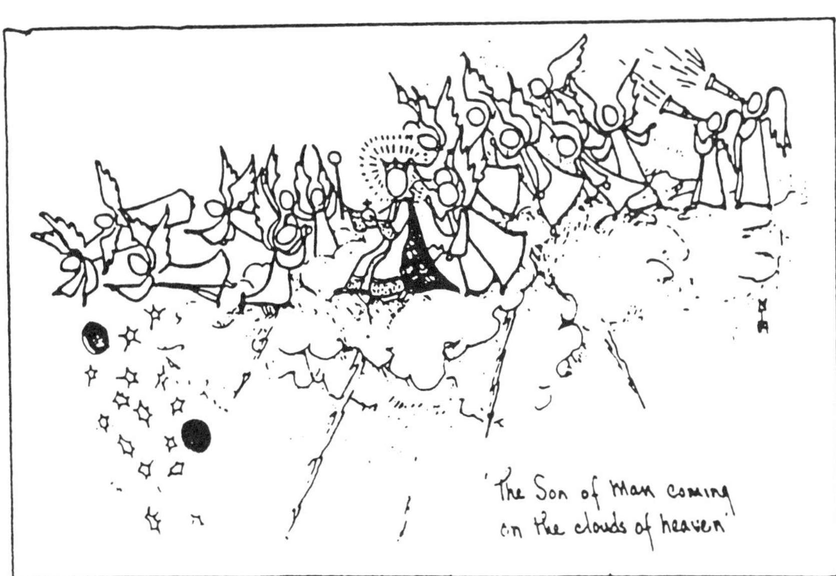


***Matthew 24:29–31***

# III.7 New Testament Letters I: 1 and 2 Timothy, Titus, James

**After studying this lesson, you will be able to:**

1. Recognize the historical, social, literary, and theological situation in the Christian communities in the latter third of the first century AD.
2. Identify the structure, date, questions of authorship, situation, and theological emphases of the Pastoral Letters.
3. Acknowledge the contribution of the Pastoral Letters in the formation of church structure.
4. Identify the structure, date, questions of authorship, situation, and theological emphases of the Letter of James.

## Read

1 and 2 Timothy, Titus, James; Kelly, pages 212–24; EDB articles: "Bishop," "Deacon, Deaconess," "Elder," "Presbyter, Presbytery," and "Widow"; "New Testament Writings: Overview—1 and 2 Timothy, Titus, James," #21 in the SUPPLEMENTARY READINGS at the back of this workbook

## Geography Task

Using the map on page 44 of your Hammond Atlas, locate Corinth, Crete, Dalmatia, Ephesus, Galatia, Macedonia, Miletus, and Thessalonica.

## Important Terms

Bishop, deacon, deaconess, elder, presbyter, widow

## Written Work

1. Answer one of the following:
   a. Compare and contrast the qualifications for the diaconate in 1 Timothy 3:8–13 with qualifications for the diaconate today.
   b. Do you think the advice given about care for widows in 1 Timothy 5:3–16 is useful today? Why or why not?

2. In what ways might 2 Timothy 3:10—4:5 help you develop your own spirituality? Be specific.

3. a. In what ways does the letter to Titus provide guidelines for Christian conduct in a Hellenistic society?
   b. Which guidelines do you think are relevant today? Why?
   c. Which guidelines do you think are not relevant today? Why?

4. How do you explain the apparent contradiction between James 2:14 and Romans 3:28 on whether we are saved by faith or by works? Be specific.

5. What do you learn from James about your use of wealth and your relationship with the poor?

## ADDITIONAL SUGGESTIONS FOR THE STUDENT

### Optional Challenges

1. How would you explain the possibility for salvation to an unmarried woman friend who read 1 Timothy 2:15? Maybe Paul himself in 1 Corinthians 7 can give you a few ideas.
2. Compare the Christian emphasis on *doing* in James 1:19–27 with that of Matthew in the Sermon on the Mount. Cite references.
3. a. What would be the characteristics of an ideal Christian for James?
   b. How do you think these characteristics apply today? Be specific.
4. Do you think the Christian community reflected in the Pastoral Letters is revolutionary in the Hellenistic culture of its time? Why or why not?
5. Is James more akin to an Old Testament prophet or a New Testament evangelist? Explain.

### Memory Verse Suggestions

I am grateful to Christ Jesus our Lord, who has strengthened me, because he judged me faithful and appointed me to his service. (1 Timothy 1:12; NRSV)

I have fought the good fight, I have finished the race, I have kept the faith. (2 Timothy 4:7; NRSV)

Avoid stupid controversies, genealogies, dissensions, and quarrels about the law, for they are unprofitable and worthless. (Titus 3:9; NRSV)

Be doers of the word, and not merely hearers who deceive themselves. (James 1:22; NRSV)

### Further Reading

*Catechism of the Catholic Church*, §4, §162, §257, §857, §1021, §1349, §1499–§1525, §1536–§1589, §1794, §1817, §1900, §2122, §2220, §2342, §2518, §2582, §2633–§2634, §2641, §2734, and §2822.

Raymond Brown, *Introduction to the New Testament* (New York: Doubleday, 1998), 638–80, 723–60.

EDB articles: "Gnosticism, Gnosis," "James, Letter of," and "Pastoral Epistles."

Kent R. Kaufman, "The Bible and Sacraments: Anointing of the Sick: A Biblical Treasure," *The Bible Today* 41, 4 (2003): 242–48.

Timothy A. Lenchak, SVD, "What's Biblical About... Anointing the Sick?" *The Bible Today* 44, 2 (2006): 111–13.

*"And they must anoint"—James 5:14*

# III.8 New Testament Letters II: 1 and 2 Peter, Jude

**After studying this lesson, you will be able to:**

1. Identify the structure, date, questions of authorship, situation, and theological emphases of 1 and 2 Peter and Jude.
2. Describe the relationship between 2 Peter and Jude.
3. Recognize the contributions of these letters in the development of Christian theology.

**Read**

1 and 2 Peter, Jude; Kelly, pages 224–31, 260–62; "New Testament Writings: Overview—1 and 2 Peter, Jude," #21 in the SUPPLEMENTARY READINGS at the back of this workbook

**Geography Task**

Using the map on page 44 in your Hammond Atlas, locate the places mentioned in 1 Peter 1:1.

**Important Term**

Baptism

**Written Work**

1. Some scholars have suggested 1 Peter may be an ancient baptismal homily.
   a. What evidence do you find in the letter itself to support or reject this claim? Cite references.
   b. How does 1 Peter enrich your own understanding of baptism? Be specific.

2. a. In 1 Peter, what images are used to describe the Christian community? Cite references.
   b. How do these images contribute to your own understanding of the Christian community?
   c. What other images might you use in describing the Christian community today?

3. 2 Peter is often thought to be the last book of the New Testament to have been written. What evidence do you find in the letter to support or reject that claim? Cite references.

4. In 2 Peter 3:1–10, how does the author help Christians deal with the delay of the coming of Jesus? Be specific.

5. a. What point is the author of Jude making in his letter?
   b. How does the author of Jude use the Old Testament and other sources to make his point?

---

*"Evangelization happens when the word of Jesus speaks to people's hearts and minds. Needing no trickery or manipulation, evangelization can happen only when people accept the Gospel freely as the 'good news' it is meant to be, because of the power of the Gospel message and the accompanying grace of God."*

*—U.S. Bishops' Letter on Evangelization, "Go and Make Disciples" (November 1992)*

## ADDITIONAL SUGGESTIONS FOR THE STUDENT

### Optional Challenges

1. Do you think the language about suffering in 1 Peter applies to a real situation of suffering or to the everyday struggle of being a Christian? Why?
2. Compare the advice to Christian slaves given in 1 Timothy 6:1–2 and 1 Peter 2:18–25. How does this advice reflect the church's stance toward the Hellenistic society of its times?

### Memory Verse Suggestions

But you are a chosen race, a royal priesthood, a holy nation, God's own people, in order that you may proclaim the mighty acts of him who called you out of darkness into his marvelous light. (1 Peter 2:9; NRSV)

Therefore, beloved, while you are waiting for these things, strive to be found by him at peace, without spot or blemish; and regard the patience of our Lord as salvation. (2 Peter 3:14–15a; NRSV)

But you, beloved, build yourselves up on your most holy faith; pray in the Holy Spirit; keep yourselves in the love of God; look forward to the mercy of our Lord Jesus Christ that leads to eternal life. (Jude 20–21; NRSV)

### Further Reading

*Catechism of the Catholic Church*, §171, §517, §554, §602, §671, §845, §1141, §1179, §1896, §1899, and §2627.

EDB articles: "Jude, Letter of," "Peter, First Letter of," and "Peter, Second Letter of."

Raymond Brown, *Introduction to the New Testament* (New York: Doubleday, 1998), 383–405, 705–24, 761–72.

Donald Senior, CP, "The Petrine Letters and The Petrine Ministry," *The Bible Today* 43, 4 (2005): 233–37.

***"Love each other intensely from the heart"***
***1 Peter 1:22***

# III.9 Hebrews

**After studying this lesson, you will be able to:**

1. Identify the structure, date, questions of authorship, situation, and theological emphases of Hebrews.
2. Recognize the contribution of Hebrews to the development of Christology, in particular the identification of Jesus as high priest of the new covenant.
3. Recognize the use of typology as a way of interpreting scripture.

## Read

Hebrews; Kelly, pages 232–38; EDB articles: "Hebrews, Epistle to the," "Melchizedek," and "Typology"; "New Testament Writings: Overview—Hebrews," #21 in the SUPPLEMENTARY READINGS at the back of this workbook

## Geography Task

Familiarize yourself with the maps of the modern world found on pages 48–51 of your Hammond Atlas.

## Important Terms

Christology, high priest, new covenant, typology

## Written Work

1. a. Identify three ways in which the author argues for the superiority of Jesus over angels (Heb 1:4—2:18). Cite references.
   b. Describe three ways in which you might argue for the superiority of Jesus over the angels.

2. a. How does the author argue for the superiority of Jesus over Moses (Heb 3:1–6)?
   b. How does Matthew 1–4 portray Jesus as a new Moses? Cite references.
   c. Is it more meaningful to you to claim that Jesus is superior to Moses or that Jesus is the new Moses? Why?

3. The author of Hebrews claims that "Indeed, the word of God is living and active, sharper than any two-edged sword, piercing until it divides soul from spirit, joints from marrow; it is able to judge the thoughts and intentions of the heart" (Heb 4:12). How have you found this to be your experience as you study the scriptures?

4. The author of Hebrews claims that "Now if he [Jesus] were on earth, he would not be a priest at all" (Heb 8:4). His high priesthood is not on earth but in heaven (Heb 8:1).
   a. Why do you think this is significant for the author?
   b. Why might it be significant for you?

5. Based on your reading of Hebrews 11–12,
   a. What is the author's definition of faith? Cite a reference.
   b. How is Abraham an example of this kind of faith? Be specific.
   c. How is Jesus an example of this kind of faith? Be specific.
   d. How does the author's definition of faith compare to your understanding of faith?

6. How does Hebrews 12:5–12 help you understand the mystery of human suffering?

**Exercise**

Note what the author considers basic Christian doctrine (Heb 6:1–2):

- Repentance from dead works
- Faith toward God
- Instruction about baptisms
- Laying on of hands
- Resurrection of the dead
- Eternal judgment

## ADDITIONAL SUGGESTIONS FOR THE STUDENT

**Optional Challenges**

1. Do you think Jeremiah would agree with the use of his new covenant quote by the author of Hebrews (Heb 8:8–13)? Why or why not?
2. a. Compare and contrast Hebrews and 1 John on the humanity of Jesus. Cite references.
   b. Which image of Jesus do you prefer? Why?
3. In what way is Jesus an *apostle* as the author of Hebrews claims (Heb 3:1)?

**Memory Verse Suggestion**

Therefore, since we are surrounded by so great a cloud of witnesses, let us also lay aside every weight and the sin that clings so closely, and let us run with perseverance the race that is set before us. (Hebrews 12:1; NRSV)

**Further Reading**

*Catechism of the Catholic Church*, §65, §102, §117, §165, §462, §609, §612, §616, §624, §635, §1009, §1137, §1165, §1364, §1476, §1540, §1564, §1820, §2100, §2188, §2568, and §2606.

Raymond Brown, *Introduction to the New Testament* (New York: Doubleday, 1998), 683–704.

*"Keep doing good works"—Hebrews 13:16*

# III.10 Unit Three Review

**You will be responsible for:**

1. A memory verse from one of the books studied in this unit, indicating the translation used and citing reference.

2. The information in the following SUPPLEMENTARY READINGS at the back of this workbook:
   #15 "The Gospel of Matthew: Overview"
   #17 "Self-Quiz: Mid-Unit Three"
   #20 "New Testament Writings: Overview"

3. The location of the following places and areas on the map "Jesus' Journey in Matthew," #16 in the SUPPLEMENTARY READINGS at the back of this workbook:
   Bethany, Bethlehem, Bethsaida, Caesarea Philippi, Capernaum, Chorazin, Decapolis, Gadara, Galilee, Gennesaret, Jerusalem, Judea, Nazareth, Sea of Galilee, Sidon, and Tyre.

***The parable of the sower—Matthew 13:4–9***

## Express your appreciation to the members of your study group

1. Take the name of one person in your small group.

2. Make sure that each person in the group has a name; contact absent members.

3. Write a brief testimonial about the gift that person's presence has been to your group during this year. Perhaps a guideline could be this message from Paul to the Ephesians (4:25–32 in part):

   *So then, putting away falsehood, let all of us speak the truth to our neighbors, for we are members of one another... Let no evil talk come out of your mouths, but only what is useful for building up, as there is need, so that your words may give grace to those who hear... and be kind to one another, tenderhearted, forgiving one another, as God in Christ has forgiven you.*

4. Bring your testimonial and share it with the group next week. After sharing with the group, present it to the person about whom you wrote.

   Reflect upon the fact that new insights about your faith journey this year have come not only from your personal study but also from working together in the group week after week. Take to heart the words of the U.S. bishops' letter on evangelization, *Go and Make Disciples* (1992):

   *Conversion is the change of our lives which comes about through the power of the Holy Spirit. All who accept the Gospel undergo a change as we continually put on the mind of Christ by rejecting sin and becoming more faithful disciples in the church. Unless we undergo conversion, we have not truly accepted the Gospel.*

# Supplementary Readings

1. The Historical Background for the Wisdom Writings: An Overview ....65
2. Wisdom in Israel: Overview ....69
3. Selections from the Instruction of Amen-em-Opet....71
4. Self-Quiz: Mid-Unit One ....73
5. Why Do Christians Have Different Bibles? ....74
6. Truth and Its Many Expressions ....79
7. Judaism in the Hellenistic World: Overview....81
8. Canon Quiz ....84
9. Who's Who in Maccabees ....86
10. Self-Quiz: Mid-Unit Two ....88
11. The Three Stages of the Composition of the Gospels (Vatican II) ....89
12. The Synoptic Gospels and Their Sources ....90
13. Material Usually Allotted to Q ....92
14. *M* Passages ....95
15. The Gospel of Matthew: Overview ....96
16. Jesus' Journey in Matthew ....98
17. Self-Quiz: Mid-Unit Three....99
18. Four Ways to Follow Jesus ....100
19. *Nostra Aetate* §4 ....106
20. The Jewish People and Their Sacred Scripture in the Christian Bible ....108
21. New Testament Writings: Overview ....111

Self-Quiz Answers....113

Four-Year Plan of Study in the Catholic Biblical School ....115

# 1. The Historical Background for the Wisdom Writings: An Overview

Anthony R. Ceresko

## Israel before the Exile

The wisdom movement and wisdom traditions in Israel reflect a clear continuity with wisdom thinking throughout the ancient world, stretching back more than two thousand years to the invention of writing, first in Mesopotamia and then in Egypt around 3000 BCE. Israel's own history begins in the thirteenth century BCE with the liberation of a number of groups from various situations of domination and oppression. These experiences were all caught up and focused in the story of the liberation of a small but important minority of what grew into "Israel" of the Tribal Confederation period, roughly 1250–1050 BCE. The model or paradigm story of the liberation of the people of Israel is the "Exodus" from Egypt of a small group of slaves under a leader named Moses.

Already clan and family wisdom had flourished for centuries among the various peoples who made up early Israel. This "popular wisdom" evolved over generations through parenting and the preparation of each new generation to cope with life and achieve some degree of success and satisfaction. From this point on, from the Exodus and the subsequent formation of "the tribes of Israel" in the hill country of Canaan, Israelite wisdom would bear the mark of the religious culture of these people. It was a religious culture characterized especially by their worship of Yahweh, the God who stands by the poor and frees the oppressed.

A new factor intervened with the arrival of David and Solomon and the establishment of a monarchy, around 1000 BCE. A new dimension of Israelite wisdom emerged that was marked specifically by its connection with writing and the concerns of court and royal temple. Scribal schools, established as a vital part of the administrative structure of palace and temple in Jerusalem, become also a forum for "wisdom thought." Contacts with international wisdom took place, and an opening up to the wisdom traditions of other peoples occurred, especially with Egypt.

Perhaps more important for us, however, was the development of an interest in creating wisdom works in written form. This interest would result during the exilic and postexilic periods in the literary works found in the Bible—Proverbs, Job, Ecclesiastes, Ben Sira, and the Wisdom of Solomon.

## The End of the Monarchy: The Destruction of Jerusalem

Toward the end of the seventh and the beginning of the sixth centuries BCE, the major Mesopotamian power of the day, Babylon, contended with Egypt for control of the border area between them. This border area included the small kingdom of Judah. The Babylonians finally gained the upper hand, and their imperial ambitions would not tolerate the least opposition or threat to their designs. They thus reacted with devastating results to crush the pretensions to autonomy and independence of the rulers and people of Judah and Jerusalem. In 587 BCE Jerusalem was destroyed, its walls pulled down, and the temple and royal palace burned to the ground. Large numbers among the leadership—the royal family and nobility, priests and temple personnel, merchants and artisans—were carried off into exile in Babylon. There they remained for the next two generations until 539 BCE.

### The Crisis of the Exile

The destruction of Jerusalem by the Babylonian armies in 587 BCE marks a dramatic turning point in Old Testament history. For six hundred years the community of Israel had enjoyed a degree of autonomy and control over its own history and future. All that came to an end with a finality that stunned and shattered this people and threatened to send them down the path to historical oblivion.

A confusion and crisis of identity followed. At one blow, all that had appeared to be at the heart of their life as a people—the holy city of Jerusalem, its temple and rich cultic traditions, and the Davidic kingship—had been brought to a brutal end. The effort to grasp what had happened, much less to begin to pick up the pieces and rebuild, was staggering. The challenge for the Jewish people during the exile and into the postexilic period was not only to survive but also to lay the groundwork for the future without abandoning their past roots. They had literally to rebuild and re-create their identity as a people.

Efforts at this re-creation and rebuilding moved in two directions. On the one hand, there was the actual physical rebuilding with the reestablishment of a Jewish community in Judah and Jerusalem. On the other hand, this rebuilding and re-creating involved an enormous literary activity which resulted in the production of large portions of what today constitutes our Bible.

### The Postexilic Restoration

The fall of the Babylonian empire to the Persians under Cyrus in 539 BCE provided the opportunity for the reestablishment of the Jewish community in Judah and Jerusalem. It was to the advantage of the Persian central administration to have a friendly and cooperative local rule in a strategically important place such as Palestine, located at the distant western end of the empire. Thus, the Persian ruler Cyrus issued a decree encouraging groups of Jews to return to their homeland and to rebuild the city of Jerusalem and its temple to their God, Yahweh.

In March of 515 BCE the new temple was dedicated, and regular conduct of the restored cult was initiated. The restoration of the temple and of a regular sacrificial ritual exercised a powerful symbolic effect for the Jewish community not only in Judah but throughout the Mediterranean world. The Jews, though many of them lived far from Judah and Jerusalem, now had a common center toward which they could turn, a symbol of hope for the future and further reestablishment.

### Jewish Identity and the Bible

The composition of the various literary works that eventually formed our Bible played an even more crucial role than the rebuilding of Jerusalem and its temple in the creation of Israel's new identity as a people.

The origins of Israel in the thirteenth century BCE coincided closely with the invention of the alphabetic script for writing. This greatly simplified form of writing facilitated the democratization of culture and thus provided a new dynamic for cultural change. Almost from the beginning, written documents played an important role in this new people's struggle to articulate their self-understanding and to safeguard for future generations their founding vision and hopes.

The people's struggle to survive and re-create their identity as Israel accelerated the production of written documents during and after the exile. The story of the monarchy had already been told in the "first edition" of the Deuteronomistic History (= the seven books from Deuteronomy through 2 Kings). This "first edition" was completed sometime between the death of King Josiah in 609 and the beginning of the exile in 587 BCE. During the exile itself this document was revised to take into account further historical developments.

More important, however, what became this community's foundational document, its Torah, or fundamental law (our Pentateuch), reached its final form, possibly by 400 BCE. The production of this document acted as something of a catalyst to crystallize and put into written form other traditional materials such as sayings and oracles of various prophets. Thus, within a century or two the Pentateuch was complemented by "the prophets." What the Jews called "the prophets" encompassed the Former Prophets, or Deuteronomistic History, and the Latter Prophets, the prophetic texts themselves. "The Law and the Prophets" would soon be spoken of in a single breath as together forming the foundation for Jewish life.

Other writings also emerged during this postexilic period, including the so-called wisdom writings of the Old Testament. The "Law and the Prophets" address more directly community concerns—the articulation of the group's identity, its origins, and the specific way of life that characterized it. The wisdom writings, on the other hand, deal with family matters and individual concerns. Taken together, these wisdom writings represent a whole array not only of "survival strategies" in the midst of the confusing and challenging postexilic world. More than that, they offer a way for the "wise" individual to live a fulfilling and satisfying life of love and loyalty to Israel's covenant God, a "spirituality" for dealing with the pressures and challenges of daily life as a faithful Jew.

### Economic and Social Disorder

Some familiarity with the social and especially economic measures imposed on the subject peoples by the successive imperial regimes can shed light on the particular challenges faced by Jews in daily life during the postexilic times... Scholars have used the word "communitarian" to describe the economic arrangements mandated by customary law.

Each extended family possessed a "house" or portion of land, an "inheritance," which was handed on from generation to generation and which guaranteed access to the basic resources needed for survival. That ancestral property was to remain within the family and was not supposed to be sold or mortgaged.

A system of "mutual aid" was in place to assist families in financial crisis—because of drought or crop failure, for example. This system required members of a clan or tribe to provide low interest loans or outright gifts to those families in crisis lest they be forced to sell or mortgage their "house."

During the monarchy this communitarian economy came into conflict with the demands of the Israelite and Judean kings for tribute in the form of taxes or forced labor. This imposition of a centralized monarchical government's tributary measures weakened but did not destroy the deeply rooted tributary-free communitarian order inherited from the earliest days of the tribal confederation. During the exilic and postexilic periods, both the Jews who remained in Palestine and those who fled or were deported drew on communitarian values and practices to survive as a people.

Nonetheless, the socioeconomic crisis deepened and further threatened these traditions. When the Persians assumed power they imposed a new system for the collection of taxes. Beginning with the reign of Darius (522–486 BCE), the Jews were required to pay their taxes no longer as a percentage of produce from their crops but in coinage. In other words, they had first to sell the produce and then with the money from the transaction pay a fixed sum to the Persian authorities in hard currency.

Times of drought or of decline in market prices proved especially difficult for the owners of small farms and their families. Many were obliged to go into debt and mortgage their property. Some were even reduced to selling themselves and/or their children into foreign slavery to pay off their debts (see Neh 5:1–5). The book of Proverbs and the book of Job both struggle with the theological and spiritual questions generated by these developments and crises...

### Alexander the Great and the Greeks

The rule of the Persians over Judah and Jerusalem came to an end with the arrival of Alexander the Great and the Greeks in 333 BCE. At the same time as the armies of Alexander were sweeping across the ancient world, the aggressive militarism of the Greeks set the stage for an unparalleled expansion of Greek commercial enterprises. Greek culture, philosophy, and religion provided powerful ideological tools both for justifying and for effecting the subjugation and exploitation of the conquered nations.

The Greek rulers after Alexander continued the earlier Persian system for siphoning off the wealth of the peoples whom they ruled by means of taxes and levies. The gap increased between the small landowners and farmers on the one hand and the rich aristocratic classes on the other. The elite ruling classes included both foreign officials based in Palestine itself or elsewhere and their upper-class Jewish agents and collaborators.

Many small farmers and their families were dispossessed of their properties while the rich, aristocratic classes accumulated ever larger tracts of land for themselves and/or as agents of foreign ruling powers. The dispossessed farmers and sheepherders now worked the land as tenant farmers or day laborers.

Within this new and expanding market economy, older values and relationships based on family and kinship ties were threatened. These ties had fostered mutual aid and support among family and kinship group members. But now people of the same family or kinship group found themselves in different and opposing economic strata. Values and older ethical standards based on human loyalty and compassion gave way to more materialistic measurements of wealth and influence with the foreign ruling power and its agents. This situation and these issues form the context and questions with which the author of Ecclesiastes (Qoheleth) deals.

### The Challenge of Greek Ways

Finally, one of the key questions the Jews had to confront after the arrival of Alexander and the Greeks was [the Jewish] stance toward Greek culture. Nor was it a purely theoretical question, or a matter of opinion or tastes. The Greek rulers would naturally favor those individuals and parties more open to Greek ways. Both as individuals and as a community, Jews had to make choices and take decisions that affected the shape and future of their culture and religion. Two of the wisdom writings in particular, Ben Sira and the Wisdom of Solomon, represent attempts to engage and respond to such issues.

We have sketched out the variety of contexts—historical, cultural, and socioeconomic—out of which Israel's scriptures emerged, including the wisdom writings. Within this wider picture, each work has its place and specific questions and issues with which it deals.

*Introduction to Old Testament Wisdom: A Spirituality for Liberation* (Maryknoll, NY: Orbis Books, 1999), 24–29. Used with permission.

*Fr. Ceresko is a professor of Old Testament at St. Peter's Pontifical Institute in Bangalore, India.*

# 2. Wisdom in Israel: Overview

*The Mystery and Mastery of Life!*

## PROVERBS

**Date:** Post-exilic

**Purpose:** Mastery of everyday life

**Themes:**

- Goal is fullness of life
- True prosperity includes material life too
- Life now is all we have
- God is an active cause of all
- God is just, rewards good and punishes evil
- The two ways: just vs. fool
- Focus on creation
- Egyptian, international influence
- Poetic parallelism
- Lady Wisdom (Prov 8)
- Brief, concise sayings about practical living

## SIRACH/ECCLESIASTICUS

(Deuterocanonical)

**Date:** Written in Jerusalem ca. 190 BC, and then translated into Greek in Egypt by his grandson ca. 132 BC

**Purpose:** Wisdom to strengthen Jews living in Hellenistic culture

**Themes:**

- Teacher becomes worshiper
- Wisdom becomes Torah
- True wisdom found in Israel
- Wisdom is an ally of Judaism in struggle for identity in Hellenistic culture
- Use of many scripture quotes
- Folly becomes "sin"
- Human freedom (Sir 15)
- Praise of God in creation (Sir 42–43)
- Praise of famous ancestors (Sir 44–50)

## WISDOM OF SOLOMON

(Deuterocanonical)

**Date:** ca. 150–50 BC

**Place:** Alexandria in Egypt

**Purpose:** Wisdom to strengthen Jews in Hellenistic society by reflection on Jewish scriptures

**Themes:**

- True wisdom found in Israel
- Immortality as reward of life in fidelity to Jewish covenant
- Revised understanding of suffering, childlessness, early death
- Hellenistic influence on the presentation of wisdom (Wis 7–8)
- Midrash on Exodus experience
- God's power and mercy/our idolatry
- Creation theology

## HABAKKUK

(One of the twelve minor prophets)

**Date:** Before the Babylonian exile, ca. 605–597 BC

**Situation:** Imminent threat to Jerusalem by the power of the Babylonians (Chaldeans)

**Themes:**

- Questioning God's inactivity
- Complaints about God's governance (Hab 1)
- Curses or woes against evildoers (Hab 2)
- Canticle (Hab 3)
- YHWH as warrior
- Memory of God's mighty deeds
- Problem of evil and God's choice of political instruments
- Call to trust, be faithful, and wait

## JOB

**Date:** An undated folktale expanded in post-exilic times

**Purpose:** A questioning of the traditional wisdom presentation of God's ways with humanity, especially retributive justice

**Themes:**

- The retributive justice of God
- Connection of suffering and sin
- God appears to be irrational, an enemy
- The ways of God the creator are ultimately a mystery
- Skepticism regarding the possibility of achieving wisdom (Job 28)
- God is free not to reveal all to Job
- God is simultaneously and mysteriously powerful, just, merciful, and free

## ECCLESIASTES/QOHELETH

**Date:** Middle post-exilic period, ca. 300–200 BC

**Purpose:** An expression of utter skepticism regarding wisdom and an awareness of the limitations of the wisdom tradition

**Themes:**

- Vanity of vanities, all is vanity (Eccl 1–6)
- Cannot know life's mysteries (Eccl 7–11)
- Challenge to traditional theology of retribution
- Pessimistic regarding the afterlife
- God is distant and impersonal
- Enjoyment of life's simple gifts and pleasures is encouraged
- In Ecclesiastes there is no afterlife; the book tends toward agnosticism and even pessimism

# 3. Selections from the Instruction of Amen-em-Opet

A general parallelism of thought or structure between Egyptian and Hebrew literature is common. It is, however, more difficult to establish a case of direct literary relation. For this reason, special attention is directed to the instruction of Amen-em-Opet, son of Ka-nakht, and its very close relation to the Book of Proverbs, particularly Proverbs 22:17—24:22. Amen-em-Opet differs from earlier Egyptian books of wisdom in its humbler, more resigned, and less materialistic outlook.

The hieratic text is found in the British Museum Papyrus 10474 and (a portion only) on a writing tablet in Turin. The papyrus is said to have come from Thebes. The date of the papyrus manuscript is debated. It is certainly subsequent to the Egyptian Empire. A date anywhere between the tenth and sixth centuries BC is possible, with some weight of evidence for the seventh through the sixth centuries.

He Says:

***First Chapter:***

Give thy ears, hear what is said,
Give thy heart to understand them.
To put them in thy heart is worth while,
(But) it is damaging to him who neglects them.
Let them rest in the casket of thy belly,
That they may be a key in thy heart...

***Ninth Chapter:***

Do not associate to thyself the heated man,
Nor visit him for conversation...

***Eighteenth Chapter:***

Do not spend the night fearful of the morrow.
At daybreak what is the morrow like?
Man knows not what the morrow is like.
God is (always) in his success,
Whereas man is in his failure;
One thing are the words which men say,
Another is that which the god does.
Say not: "I have no wrongdoing,"
Nor (yet) strain to seek quarreling.
As for wrongdoing, it belongs to the god;
It is sealed with his finger.
There is no success in the hand of the god,
But there is no failure before him.
If he pushes himself to seek success,
In the completion of a moment he damages it.
Be steadfast in thy heart, make firm thy breast.
Steer not thy tongue (alone).
If the tongue of a man (be) the rudder of a boat,
The All-Lord is its pilot...

***Twenty-Third Chapter:***

Do not eat bread before a noble,
Nor lay on thy mouth at first.
If thou art satisfied with false chewings,
They are a pastime for thy spittle.

Look at the cup which is before thee,
And let it serve thy needs.
As a noble is great in his office,
He is as a well abounds (in) the drawing (of water)...

***Thirtieth Chapter:***

See thou these thirty chapters:
They entertain; they instruct;
They are the foremost of all books;
They make the ignorant to know.
If they are read out before the ignorant,
Then he will be cleansed by them.
Fill thyself with them; put them in thy heart,
And be a man who can interpret them,
Who will interpret them as a teacher.
As for the scribe who is experienced in his office,
He will find himself worthy (to be) a courtier...

*Ancient Near Eastern Texts*, ed. James B. Pritchard (Princeton, NJ: Princeton University Press, 1969, pp. 421–24). Used with permission.

# 4. Self-Quiz: Mid-Unit One

1. Identify the name of the biblical book from this unit that best matches the description.

Proverbs
Habakkuk
Job

_______________ a. Hero of this story questions God's retributive justice

_______________ b. Calls to trust, fidelity, and waiting

_______________ c. Early post-exilic collection of sayings providing guidance for everyday living

_______________ d. Classified as one of the minor prophets

_______________ e. Combines a folktale and a poetic dialogue

_______________ f. Shares similarities with Amen-em-Opet

_______________ g. Challenges Deuteronomic vision of God in a dialogue with friends

_______________ h. Book that personifies and contrasts Wisdom and Folly as two women

2. Who is the patron of Old Testament wisdom literature?

3. What do you think is an important contribution of wisdom literature?

4. Be sure you can locate the land of Chaldeans and the city of Alexandria on a map.

*(Answers to quiz can be found on page 113)*

# 5. Why Do Christians Have Different Bibles?

**Daniel F. Stramara, OSB**

Scene at a hypothetical Bible study on repentance:

A Protestant believer has just declared, "I don't need to repent anymore now that I've accepted Jesus." A Catholic participant responds by quoting from Sirach: "He who fears the Lord constantly bears about repentance in his heart" (21:6). Puzzled, the Protestant rejoins, "That's not in my Bible!"

Trying to be helpful, an Orthodox member reads from her Bible. "I found an illuminating passage from the Prayer of Manasseh: 'Therefore, You O Lord, God of Righteousness, have not appointed repentance for the righteous such as Abraham, Isaac, and Jacob who did not sin against you, but for me a sinner in need of repentance.'" With eyebrows raised, the Protestant and Catholic exchange glances of bewilderment.

A brown-skinned man with a foreign accent chimes in with a verse from 1 Enoch: "Then Wisdom shall be given to the elect of God. And they shall have a life and sin no more, either by being wicked or through vainglory; those who possess Wisdom shall be humble and sin no more" (5:8).

The group falls silent, utterly amazed that books they've never even heard of before are being quoted as Scripture.

Why *do* Christians have different Bibles? In this article I hope to make a brief, unbiased survey as to how this all came about.

### The Jews and Their Bible

In order to understand Christian Bibles, it is first necessary to take a look at the Jewish Bible. It is divided into three sections: the Law, the Prophets, and the Writings. The Law consists of the five books of Moses (Genesis to Deuteronomy). These formed the core of the *canon*. *Canon* is a Greek word meaning "reed," "measuring rod." The Law, therefore, was the canon, the measuring rod by which all later works were judged for correctness.

The next Jewish division of the OT (Old Testament) is the Prophets. This section contains books written by prophets like Isaiah, Jeremiah, etc., and books telling about the activities of prophets, such as the Books of Samuel.

The last division of the OT is the Writings, a quite diversified group, including, for example, Psalms, Proverbs, Ruth, and the apocalyptic work of Daniel. As centuries went by, the number of books in the Writings increased.

### What Is the Septuagint?

The Septuagint (from the Greek meaning "seventy") is a Greek translation of the Hebrew Bible as well as other Jewish religious writings that are no longer part of the present-day Hebrew Bible. The Septuagint (abbreviated by its Roman numerals LXX) is the work of many translators. It was produced in the third and second centuries BC for Greek-speaking Jews. The LXX has more books in the section known as the Writings than the modern Hebrew Bible.

### What Bible Did Jesus and His Disciples Use?

Strictly speaking, there was no "Bible" then as we have it today. The canon wasn't closed or fixed during Jesus' lifetime. There was no authoritative list. Hence, many of Jesus' sayings are influenced by the Book of Sirach (not found in the Hebrew Bible, but part of the LXX). Any scholarly, objective approach to the NT (New Testament) substantiates numerous parallels to the "extra" books contained in the LXX. The earliest Apostolic Fathers freely quote from the whole of the LXX as being inspired.

### When Did the Jews Close Their Canon?

Around AD 100 rabbis held a council at Jamnia, Israel. Since the Temple had been destroyed in AD 70, Jews needed to secure their identity, especially in opposition to Jews believing in Jesus as Messiah. It is believed that at this meeting they decided on the present-day Jewish Bible. However, the authority of such books as Esther, Proverbs, Song of Songs, Ruth, Ecclesiastes, and Ezekiel were challenged at the meeting and even later. Even the Book of Sirach, supposedly rejected at the council, was quoted by rabbis as inspired for centuries afterward.

When any people is persecuted, it naturally regroups and stresses its national history and language. Thus in AD 130, after much foreign oppression, the rabbis forbade Jews to read the Scriptures in Greek from the LXX. Jews were to read the Hebrew text only. Furthermore, Christians had been quoting the LXX to win converts; Jews could refute their arguments on the basis of a "faulty translation." By thus emphasizing Hebrew language and tradition, the rabbis preserved Jewish social identity.

### How Then Did the Church Decide Which OT Books to Accept?

From AD 90 onward, Christian writers explicitly quote from the "extra books" of the LXX. When the NT quotes the OT, 85 percent of the time it is from the LXX. But in the second century, as Christians debated with Jews trying to convert them, they needed to meet them on their own ground, i.e., the Hebrew canon. As certain Church Fathers stopped using the extra books in debates, some Christians came to doubt their inspiration. However, facts show that when these same Church Fathers taught in their own circles, they employed the full LXX.

The Septuagint was accepted as the official and inspired version of the OT because of its long-standing and consistent use by the apostles and their disciples. In 393 St. Augustine and the Council of Hippo approved the list of books as contained in the present Catholic Bible. This was likewise ratified at Carthage in 397 and 419 and by the church practices of Rome.

### Then Why Do Christians Have Different Old Testaments?

The early Christian Church was Greek-speaking; it therefore used the LXX. Even though the LXX sometimes gave different readings from the original Hebrew and had "extra books" *interspersed* with the rest, the early Church believed it to be inspired. "With regard to whatever is in the Septuagint that is not in the Hebrew manuscripts, we can say that the one Spirit wished to say to them through the writers of the former rather than through the latter in order to show that both the one and the other were inspired" (St. Augustine, *City of God* 18:43).

Hence the Orthodox Church uses only the LXX and not the original Hebrew as the official inspired OT. The LXX, compared to the Hebrew Bible, has the following additional books: Tobit, Judith, Wisdom, Sirach, Baruch (including the Letter of Jeremiah), 1–3 Maccabees, Prayer of Manasseh, Psalm 151, 1 Esdras, additions to Esther and Daniel, and, very rarely, 4 Maccabees. The Orthodox Church, however, never accepted 4 Maccabees, since it wasn't widely available and was never considered inspired.

Since the Christians in the West spoke Latin, they translated the Bible into Latin, beginning about AD 150. But this was *first* of all done from the LXX, *not* the Hebrew. It wasn't until the end of the fourth century that St. Jerome made a translation from the Hebrew. It was then that he discovered that the Jews had a different Bible. Believing that Jesus never used anything other than the Hebrew Bible, Jerome wished to adopt their canon. Modern historical studies have shown, however, that the Jews did in fact have these other books and read them during Christ's time. Jerome was merely ill-informed, and the Tradition of the Church prevailed. Hence the Latin Bible (known as the *Vulgate*) contained the same books as the LXX.

Increasingly, copies of the Latin Bible dropped out 1 Esdras, 3 Maccabees, the Prayer of Manasseh, and Psalm 151. Consequently, when the Catholic Church responded to Protestantism at the Council of Trent, the Latin Vulgate that it made official on April 8, 1546, did not include these four works.

Protestantism, initiated by Martin Luther, accepted the Jewish canon. Like Jerome, believing that Jesus used only the Hebrew Bible, Luther excluded the additional books found in the LXX. He also rejected the role of Oral Tradition as being equally authoritative with Scripture. Hence he questioned the Church's right to say which books were canonical. He himself, though, repudiated Esther and James and looked askance at the Book of Revelation. Had Protestantism followed Luther's preferences in the NT, Christendom would not only have different Old Testaments, but different New Testaments as well.

Besides Catholics, Orthodox, and Protestants having varying Old Testaments, the unfortunately forgotten and yet venerable Coptic and Ethiopian Churches include one book more than the Orthodox: the Book of Enoch. The Letter of Jude 14–15 is a direct quote from 1 Enoch 1:9. Scholarship has shown that the Book of Enoch also influenced at least fifteen other NT books. It was widely used and up until the fourth century and considered by numerous Church Fathers to be inspired. The West lost it because it was never translated into Latin. Later in the East it also fell into disuse because of some heretical misuse.

Because of local church councils and differences in language, coupled later on with a lack of historical criticism and knowledge, modern Christendom now has four Old Testaments.

### What Are the Disputed Books Called?

Quite frankly, it's a bit confusing and you need a chart! In the chart on page 77, column 1 shows the Protestant listing. Whatever books of the LXX are not part of the Hebrew Bible, the Protestants call *Apocrypha*, meaning "hidden." Anything outside of the LXX, Protestants call *Pseudepigrapha*, meaning "false writings"

Catholics call the books accepted by the Jews *Protocanonical*, meaning the "first canon." The others listed form the *Deutrocanonical* books, the "second canon." All the rest they call *Apocrypha*.

The Orthodox follow suit but have additional books in the list of *Deuterocanonicals*. Anything not found in the LXX is called *Apocrypha*.

Coptics would group 1 Enoch along with the Deuterocanonical books and call any other ancient writings Apocrypha.

### But, Thank God, We All Have the Same New Testament!

Well... it wasn't until the end of the fifth century that all Christians had the same NT. Out of the many books in circulation, different provinces accepted various canons. The Church approved a book if it was apostolic in its origin. That doesn't mean that it literally had to be written by an apostle, but that it was influenced by him and his followers. Tradition was primary in the formation of the canon of the Bible. Thus, the Church accepted

| PROTESTANT | CATHOLIC | ORTHODOX | COPTIC |
|---|---|---|---|
| Law<br>Prophets<br>Writings | PROTOCANONICAL | PROTOCANONICAL | PROTOCANONICAL |
| APOCRYPHA | Tobit<br>Judith<br>Wisdom<br>Sirach<br>Baruch<br>1 & 2 Maccabees<br>Additions to Esther<br>Additions to Daniel | DEUTEROCANONICAL | |
| | | 3 Maccabees<br>Prayer of Manasseh<br>Psalm 151<br>1 Esdras | |
| | APOCRYPHA | | 1 Enoch |
| PSEUDEPIGRAPHA | | APOCRYPHA | APOCRYPHA<br>(4 Maccabees, etc.) |

the Gospel of Luke and the Acts [of the Apostles] on the basis of Luke's being a disciple of Paul. The Gospel of Mark records the teachings of Peter.

Some churches, however, didn't know to whom to attribute books such as Hebrews or Revelation. The East accepted Hebrews as Pauline; the West rejected it. The West accepted Revelation as from the Apostle John; the East rejected it. 2 Peter and 2–3 John, James, and Jude, endured prolonged scrutiny and doubt. 1–2 Timothy and Titus faced only some questioning. Certain churches, however, accepted other works attributed to Paul. The Syrian Church accepted a third letter to the Corinthians until the fifth century. The West also employed an Epistle to the Laodiceans for a short time.

But besides these writings, still others were considered inspired in various places and at different times, such as: 1 Clement, Didache, Shepherd of Hermas, Apocalypse of Peter, and Barnabas.

**How Was the Problem Solved?**

The test of Apostolic Tradition was the main factor. Could the book be ascribed to some apostle or group of disciples? Also, was the book *widely* used and accepted throughout *all* of Christendom? Hence, 1 Clement even though internally claiming inspiration and being acclaimed as inspired by some churches, wasn't used everywhere and therefore was not held to be canonical. That's not to say it couldn't be inspired, but rather the book isn't *normative*. Canonicity and inspiration are two different things.

**What's Become of These Other Books?**

First of all, let me make a list of books so we know what we're talking about: 1 Enoch, 3 Maccabees, Prayer of Manasseh, 1 Esdras, Psalm 151, 1 Clement, Didache, Shepherd of Hermas,

3 Corinthians, and Apocalypse of Peter. These works still exist today. At one time they were considered to be inspired and canonical. Some, as explained above, still are so considered. Anyone can read these and spiritually profit by them. I know I have. These books are witnesses to, and help make up, what we call Tradition. They are testimonies of the Holy Spirit working in the People of God.

Several *inspired* books are now lost and not part of the Bible. For example, the Books of Jashar (Jos 10:13; 2 Sam 1:18), of the Prophet Nathan (1 Chr 29:29; 2 Chr 9:29), of the Prophet Gad (1 Chr 29:29), and the Scripture behind James 4:5, just to mention a few. The canon is a rule of thumb, a guideline, a measuring rod. Not everything that is inspired is in the canon; but everything in the canon is inspired. When Jesus spoke, his words were inspired and authoritative. But not all of his words were written down. That is why Oral Tradition is so very important. Whether one accepts the aforementioned books as canonical or not, they are still part of Tradition, which is equally authoritative. Yet they, like Scripture, are to be interpreted only within and by the one, holy, catholic, apostolic Church, for they came forth from her.

### Objections Often Raised

Some reject the extra books because they are never quoted verbatim in the NT. In that case, however, one should also exclude Esther and Nahum, etc., for they too are never *directly* quoted.

Others cite Revelation 22:18 as proof that one cannot add books to or delete them from the Bible. This verse, though, applies only to tampering with the Book of Revelation. Besides, the Gospel of John, 1–3 John, and 2 Peter were written after the Book of Revelation was completed.

### Well, Is the Canon Closed?

For a Catholic, technically, "no." The Council of Trent only specified which books were definitely inspired, though indeed the Church has said certain books are heretical. Thus Catholics could eventually have the same canon as the Orthodox and even Coptic Churches. There is much room for Christian dialogue.

But what is most important is that the Word of God became flesh in us just as it did in the Virgin Mary. "Clearly you are a letter of Christ... a letter written not with ink but by the Spirit of the Living God, not on tablets of stone but on tablets of flesh in the heart" (2 Cor 3:3). How clearly *do* we reflect the Word who is Life? Do we clearly hear the voice of the Holy Spirit in whatever canon we possess? If we as Christians concern ourselves with these questions, then I believe one day we will be one Church with one Bible.

# 6. Truth and Its Many Expressions

## Vatican II on How to Interpret the Scriptures:

### Excerpts from the Dogmatic Constitution on Divine Revelation (*Dei Verbum*)

§10. Sacred tradition and sacred Scripture form one sacred deposit of the word of God, which is committed to the Church. Holding fast to this deposit, the entire holy people united with their shepherds remain always steadfast in the teaching of the apostles, in the common life, in the breaking of the bread, and in prayers, so that in holding to, practicing, and professing the heritage of the faith, there results on the part of the bishops and faithful a remarkable common effort.

The task of authentically interpreting the word of God, whether written or handed on, has been entrusted exclusively to the living teaching office of the Church, whose authority is exercised in the name of Jesus Christ. This teaching office is not above the word of God, but serves it, teaching only what has been handed on, listening to it devoutly, guarding it scrupulously, and explaining it faithfully by divine commission and with the help of the Holy Spirit; it draws from this one deposit of faith everything which it presents for belief as divinely revealed.

It is clear, therefore, that sacred tradition, sacred Scripture, and the teaching authority of the Church, in accord with God's most wise design, are so linked and joined together that one cannot stand without the others, and that all together and each in its own way under the action of the one Holy Spirit contribute effectively to the salvation of souls.

**CHAPTER 3. SACRED SCRIPTURE: ITS DIVINE INSPIRATION AND ITS INTERPRETATION**

§11. Those divinely revealed realities which are contained and presented in sacred Scripture have been committed to writing under the inspiration of the Holy Spirit. Holy Mother Church, relying on the belief of the apostles, holds that the books of both the Old and New Testament in their entirety, with all their parts, are sacred and canonical because, having been written under the inspiration of the Holy Spirit they have God as their author and have been handed on as such to the Church herself. In composing the sacred books, God chose men and while employed by God they made use of their powers and abilities, so that with God acting in them and through them, they, as true authors, consigned to writing everything and only those things which God wanted.

Therefore, since everything asserted by the inspired authors or sacred writers must be held to be asserted by the Holy Spirit, it follows that the books of Scripture must be acknowledged as teaching firmly, faithfully, and without error that truth which God wanted put into the sacred writings for the sake of our salvation. Therefore, "all Scripture is inspired by God and useful for teaching, for reproving, for correcting, for instruction in justice; that the man of God may be perfect, equipped for every good work" (2 Tim 3:16–17).

§12. However, since God speaks in sacred Scripture through men in human fashion, the interpreter of sacred Scripture, in order to see clearly what God wanted to communicate to us, should carefully investigate what **meaning** the sacred writers really intended, and what God wanted to manifest by means of their words.

Those who search out the intention of the sacred writers must, among other things, have regard for the **literary forms**. For truth is proposed and expressed in a variety of ways, depending on whether a text is history of one kind or another, or whether its form is that of prophecy, poetry, or some other type of speech.

The interpreter must investigate what meaning the sacred writer intended to express and actually expressed in particular circumstances as he used contemporary literary forms in accordance with the situation of his own time and culture.

For the correct understanding of what the sacred author wanted to assert, due attention must be paid to the **customary and characteristic styles of perceiving, speaking, and narrating** which prevailed at the time of the sacred writer, and to the **customs people normally followed at that period** in their everyday dealings with one another.

But, since holy Scripture must be read and interpreted according to the same Spirit by whom it was written, no less serious attention must be given to the content and unity of the whole of Scripture, if the meaning of the sacred texts is to be correctly brought to light. The living tradition of the whole Church must be taken into account along with the harmony which exists between elements of the faith. It is the task of exegetes to work according to these rules toward a better understanding and explanation of the meaning of Sacred Scripture, so that through preparatory study the judgment of the Church may mature.

For all of what has been said about the way of interpreting scripture is subject finally to the judgment of the Church, which carries out the divine commission and ministry of guarding and interpreting the word of God.

## AN APPLICATION FOR OUR OWN SCRIPTURAL EXEGESIS

The goal of scripture study is the understanding of ***MEANING***, which demands locating a text within its contexts, moving beyond simple facts to also indicate their significance.

The first step recognizes the ***LITERARY CONTEXT***. We must learn to read the texts according to the best methods of interpretation of literature, and in particular we must not confuse types of literature.

The second step recognizes the ***HISTORICAL CONTEXT***. We must learn to interpret texts in their own historical time and in the specific situations in which they were composed.

The third step recognizes the ***SOCIAL (CULTURAL) AND RHETORICAL CONTEXT***. We must learn to recognize the cultural situation out of which the texts came and for which they were a response in accord with the communication needs of the original audience.

For the full understanding (exegesis) of the meaning of a text, all of these methods must be used. But after our exegesis, we must finally make the ***APPLICATION*** of this meaning to our situation today. This application is essential, and can be done well only if we have considered as thoroughly as possible what the text meant to the original audience and in the living tradition of the church community. We must also carefully examine our own presuppositions for applying the text.

# 7. Judaism in the Hellenistic World: Overview

## JONAH

(One of the twelve minor prophets)

**Date:** Persian period

**Situation:** Addresses the narrowmindedness and rigidity of the people and their excessive nationalism

**Literary Style:** Didactic fiction

**Themes:**
- Conversion
- Role of the prophet/response to call
- God's mercy and justice
- Openness to those who are different

## ESTHER

(With deuterocanonical additions)

**Date:** Post-exilic

**Situation:** Life in the diaspora

**Literary Style:** Didactic fiction

**Themes:**
- Reversals
- Providence of God
- Response to persecution
- Living in an alien culture
- God not named in Hebrew version
- Prayer added in deuterocanonical text
- Purim

## TOBIT

(Deuterocanonical)

**Date:** Greek period, ca. 200–180 BC

**Situation:** Life in the diaspora

**Literary Style:** Didactic fiction

**Themes:**
- Hero's journey
- Marriage/family
- The just person
- Angels
- Identity in the diaspora

## BARUCH

(Deuterocanonical)

**Date:** Greek period

**Situation:** Life in the diaspora

**Literary Style:** Mixture of prose, wisdom, poetry, lament, letter

**Themes:**
- Spirituality for the diaspora
- Prayer, need for conversion
- Jewish wisdom gives life
- Jerusalem focus
- Against idolatry
- Pseudonymous authorship

## 1 MACCABEES

(Deuterocanonical)

**Date:** ca. 100 BC

**Situation:** Jewish resistance to Seleucid ruler, Antiochus IV Epiphanes, and later Jewish independence

**Literary Style:** Historical narrative; original composition

**Themes:**

- Response to persecution
- Reaction against Hellenism
- Fidelity to Yahweh and Torah
- Desecration and restoration of temple
- Military response of the Maccabees
- Pro-Hasmonean viewpoint

## 2 MACCABEES

(Deuterocanonical)

**Date:** after 124 BC

**Situation:** Interpretation of Maccabean revolt for Egyptian Jews

**Literary Style:** History with a theological emphasis; summary of a larger five-volume work

**Themes:**

- Observance of Law
- Deuteronomic emphasis
- Resurrection of the body
- Martyrdom
- Angels
- Prayer for the dead
- Intercession of the saints
- Temple and its holiness
- Hanukkah

## JUDITH

(Deuterocanonical)

**Date:** ca. 150 BC

**Situation:** Response to persecution

**Literary Style:** Didactic fiction

**Themes:**
- God's providence
- Victory of Yahweh over power of evil
- In human weakness is God's strength
- "Exodus" pattern
- Human response
- Trust in God
- Prayer/action
- Women in Old Testament

## DANIEL

(With deuterocanonical additions)

**Date:** ca. 165 BC during Maccabean revolt

**Situation:** Jewish life under domination of an oppressive foreign power

**Literary Style:** Mixed collection of didactic fiction—folktales chapters 1-6, 13-14; apocalyptic-visions and interpretations chapters 7-12

**Themes:**
- Tales for edification and encouragement
- Fidelity to the Law
- Loyalty to Yahweh
- Apocalyptic form of expression
- God's plan
- Angels
- Eventual triumph of God's kingdom and destruction of the earthly kingdoms
- Ideas of kingdom of God and Son of Man influential in the New Testament

# 8. Canon Quiz

For numbers 1–8, indicate whether each statement is TRUE or FALSE

__________ 1. The word *canon* originally meant a measuring stick.

__________ 2. The Council of Trent established a new canon.

__________ 3. The Jews came to accept first the Law, then the Prophets, and finally the Writings as scripture.

__________ 4. The word *canon* when applied to scriptures, means the collection of books that the church accepts as inspired and normative.

__________ 5. The Septuagint, which was produced in the area of Alexandria in Egypt, is a Syriac translation of the Old Testament.

__________ 6. The New Testament writers always quote from the Hebrew version of the Old Testament books, never from the Septuagint.

__________ 7. Protestants use the term *apocrypha* to refer to all the books in the Septuagint that are not in the Hebrew Bible.

__________ 8. Some non-canonical books that imitate the style of the Bible are called *apocrypha* by Catholics and *pseudepigrapha* by Protestants.

9. List the seven deuterocanonical books.

1. ______________________________ 5. ______________________________

2. ______________________________ 6. ______________________________

3. ______________________________ 7. ______________________________

4. ______________________________

10. How do scholars abbreviate *Septuagint*? Why?

11. A list of books considered to constitute the Bible is called the ____________.

12. The books that are part of the Catholic Bible but not part of the Protestant Bible are called by Catholics the ____________ books.

13. Protestants call these same books (see question 12) the ________________.

14. Books that are not in either the Catholic or the Protestant canons are called by both Catholics and Protestants ______________________.

15. The Deuterocanonical books were part of the Greek version of scripture called the ______________, which was used by Greek-speaking Jews and by the early Christian Church.

16. The Jewish canon was established at a gathering of rabbis at ________________ in Palestine.

17. These Palestinian rabbis rejected from the canon books written in __________ and the books that they believed to be of recent date.

18. At the time of the Reformation, after much debate, the reformed churches decided to accept the _____________ canon rather than the _____________ canon.

19. How would the following books be described by Catholics and by Protestants?

| | Catholics | Protestants |
|---|---|---|
| Ecclesiastes | ____________________ | ____________________ |
| Wisdom | ____________________ | ____________________ |
| 2 Samuel | ____________________ | ____________________ |
| Ecclesiasticus | ____________________ | ____________________ |
| 3 Maccabees | ____________________ | ____________________ |

20. The deuterocanonical books form a kind of bridge between the Hebrew Old Testament and the New Testament because they come from the period when Judaism was dealing with the _____________ culture.

*(Answers for the quiz may be found on page 113)*

# 9. Who's Who in Maccabees

**Alexander the Great:**
Son of Philip of Macedon. Reigned from 333 to 323 BC. He conquered the Persian Empire and extended his empire all the way to India. At his death, his empire was divided and eventually controlled by Ptolemy and Seleucus.

**Alexander:**
Called Balas and Epiphanes, he was a son of Antiochus IV (Epiphanes) (1 Macc 10) who named Jonathan as Jewish high priest.

**Alcimus:**
The Jewish high priest who supported the Seleucids.

**Antiochus:**
The name of several Seleucid rulers, in particular Antiochus IV called Epiphanes, emperor from 175 to 163 BC who waged a military campaign against the Jews from 168 to 165. He conquered Jerusalem and desecrated the temple.

**Cleopatra:**
Name of several Egyptian queens and princesses. The one mentioned in 1 Maccabees 10 is Cleopatra Thea, who married Demetrius II.

**Demetrius:**
The name of several Seleucid rulers, including Demetrius I Soter (162 to 150), a son of Antiochus IV who continued the struggle with the Maccabees, and Demetrius II Nicator (146 to 138), whose troops were defeated by Jonathan.

**Eleazar:**
Several people with this name appear. One is a martyr under Antiochus IV (2 Macc 6). Another is a son of Mattathias. Another killed an elephant in battle (1 Macc 6:43–46). Another is the father of the Jason sent to Rome (1 Macc 8:17).

**Hasideans:**
In Hebrew the word is *Hasidim* (i.e., "pious ones"). A devout group of Jews who espoused the strict observance of the Jewish Law. They supported the Maccabean revolt (1 Macc 2:42). Many scholars link them to the later Pharisees.

**Hasmoneans:**
The name given to the Jewish rulers from the Maccabean family that was in power from the Maccabean revolt to the conquest by the Romans in 63 BC. The Jewish historian Josephus identifies Hasmon as the father of Mattathias.

**Jason:**
Several people with this name appear. One is the author of the five-volume work of which 2 Maccabees is a condensed version (2 Macc 2:23). Another paid bribes for the high priesthood (2 Macc 4:7). Another was sent to Rome to make a treaty (1 Macc 8:17).

**John:**
John Gaddis was a son of Mattathias. John (Hyrcanus) was a grandson.

**Jonathan:**
A son of Mattathias who led the revolt from 160 to 142 and became high priest.

**Judas:**
Nicknamed "Maccabeus" (the Hammer), a son of Mattathias who led the revolt from 166 to 160.

**Mattathias:**
A devout Jewish priest whose resistance triggered the revolt that was then led by his five sons.

**Menelaus:**
Bribed his way into the high priesthood and replaced Jason (2 Macc 4).

**Ptolemy:**
Name of several rulers of the Ptolemaic Dynasty that ruled from Alexandria, Egypt. Ptolemy I founded the dynasty after Alexander the Great's death.

**Seleucus:**
Name of several rulers in the Seleucid Dynasty that ruled from Antioch in Syria. Seleucus I founded the dynasty after Alexander the Great's death.

**Simon:**
A son of Mattathias who led the revolt from 142 to 134 and became high priest. Another Simon is mentioned as temple administrator (2 Macc 3:4).

**Trypho:**
Seleucid official and army commander who seized the throne (1 Macc 13).

# 10. Self-Quiz: Mid-Unit Two

1. Identify the name of the biblical book that best matches the description.

Jonah
Esther
Tobit
Baruch
1 Maccabees
2 Maccabees

_______________ a. A historical narrative that focuses on the military response of Mattathias and his sons to the persecution of Antiochus IV

_______________ b. A story that focuses on Jewish family life in the diaspora

_______________ c. Authorship of this book is attributed to Jeremiah's secretary

_______________ d. The story of a reluctant prophet

_______________ e. A book that expresses a belief in resurrection

_______________ f. Addresses the narrow-mindedness, rigidity, and excessive nationalism of the people

_______________ g. A young man in this story goes out on a hero's journey

_______________ h. The name of God is not mentioned in the Hebrew version of this book

_______________ i. A story about deliverance from persecution in the diaspora

_______________ j. Includes a reference to prayer for the dead

2. Briefly describe the biblical story or event on which the feasts of Purim and Hanukkah are based.

3. Compare and contrast 1 and 2 Maccabees. How are they similar to and different from one another?

4. Describe Hellenism.

*(Answers to quiz can be found on page 114)*

# 11. The Three Stages of the Composition of the Gospels (Vatican II)

**STAGE 1: THE LIVED GOSPEL**

Holy Mother Church has firmly and with absolute constancy held, and continues to hold, that the four gospels just named, whose historical character the Church unhesitatingly asserts, faithfully hand on what Jesus Christ, while living among us, really did and taught for our eternal salvation until the day He was taken up into heaven (see Acts 1:1–2).

**STAGE 2: THE ORAL GOSPEL**

Indeed, after the ascension of the Lord the apostles handed on to their hearers what He had said and done. This they did with that clearer understanding which they enjoyed after they had been instructed by the events of Christ's risen life and taught by the light of the Spirit of truth.

**STAGE 3: THE WRITTEN GOSPELS**

The sacred authors wrote the four gospels, selecting some things from the many which had been handed on by word of mouth or in writing, reducing some of them to a synthesis, explaining some things in view of the situation of their churches, and preserving the form of proclamation but always in such a fashion that they told us the honest truth about Jesus. For their intention in writing was that either from their own memory and recollections, or from the witness of those who themselves "from the beginning were eyewitnesses and ministers of the word" we might know "the truth" concerning those matters about which we have been instructed (see Luke1:2–4).

—from the Dogmatic Constitution on Divine Revelation (*Dei Verbum*), §19

We must always remember these stages of composition for the gospels in order to interpret them correctly. If we understand what is described above about the process of composition, we will never confuse the gospels with eyewitness or "earwitness" recordings of the life and words of Jesus. The gospels are narrative proclamations of the good news of our salvation—the Christian gospel that Jesus of Nazareth lived, suffered, died, and rose from the dead and this is indeed our salvation. This truth is the constant factor in every genuine Christian proclamation of the gospels, no matter what form—living example, oral preaching, or written texts—the message takes.

# 12. The Synoptic Gospels and Their Sources

## DIAGRAM OF THE GOSPEL SOURCES

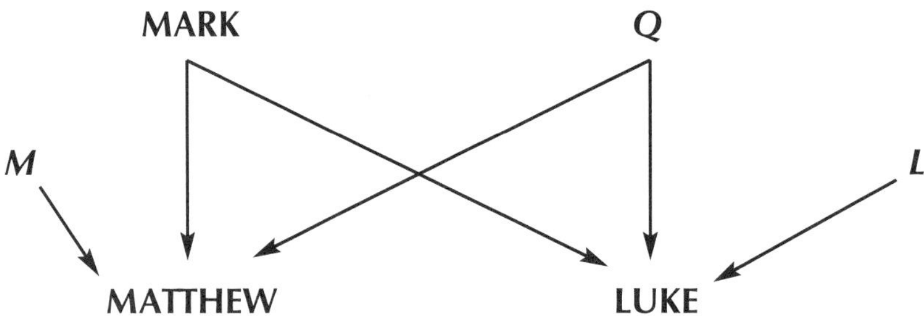


The Gospels of Mark, Matthew, and Luke are called synoptic because they can be viewed together and compared easily in parallel columns. In fact, there are certain passages that are so similar that it is clear one gospel writer copied from another. Most scholars accept *Markan Priority*, which means that Mark wrote his gospel first and that both Matthew and Luke independently used Mark as a source. The *Q* material (*Quelle*—meaning "source") refers to that which Matthew and Luke have in common but is not in Mark (e.g., the Our Father), whereas the designations *M* and *L* refer respectively to what Matthew and Luke have that is unique.

For more information about the synoptic problem, see Kelly (*An Introduction to the New Testament for Catholics*), pages 110–12. The charts on the next page represent visually the dependence of Matthew and Luke on Mark.

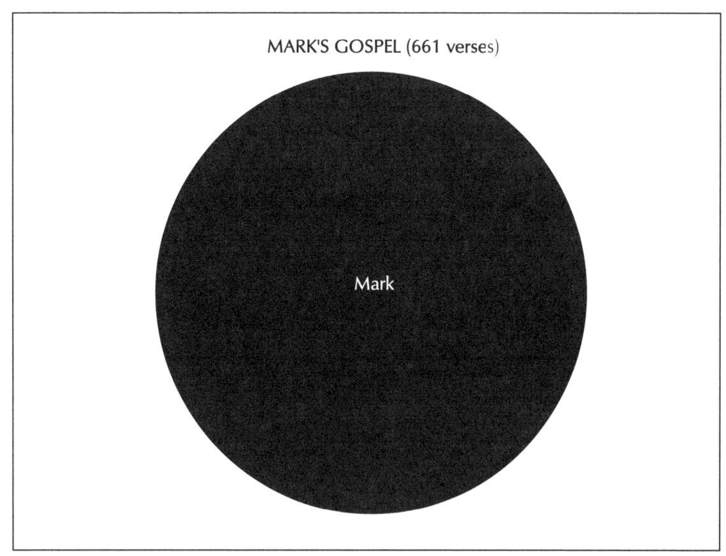
MARK'S GOSPEL (661 verses)
Mark

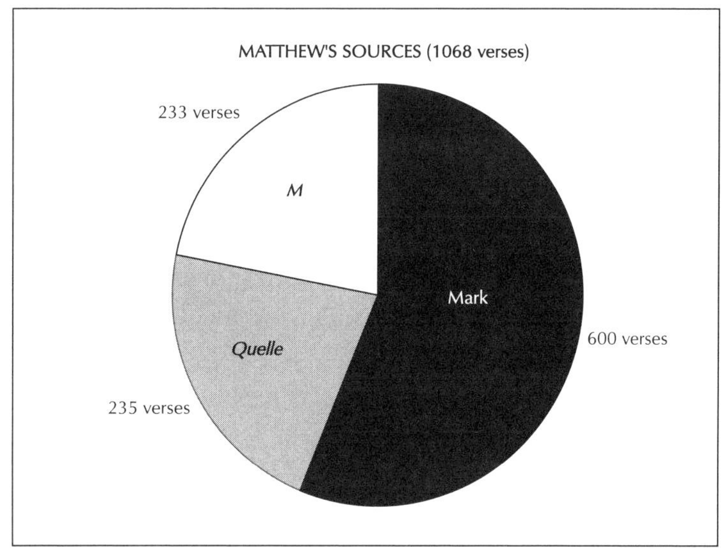
MATTHEW'S SOURCES (1068 verses)
233 verses
M
Mark
600 verses
Quelle
235 verses

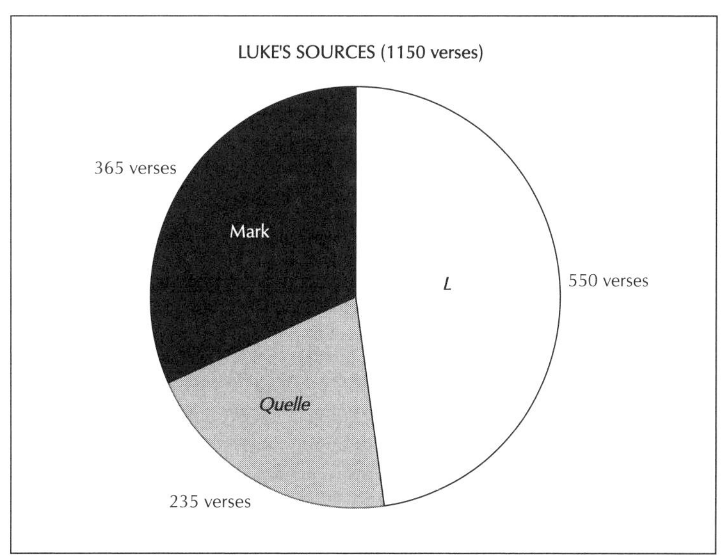
LUKE'S SOURCES (1150 verses)
365 verses
Mark
L
550 verses
Quelle
235 verses

# 13. Material Usually Allotted to *Q*

**Raymond E. Brown**

| MATTHEW | LUKE | CONTENTS |
|---|---|---|
| 3:7b–12 | 3:7–9, 16–17 | John the Baptist (JBap): warnings, promise of one to come |
| 4:2b–11a | 4:2–13 | Three temptations (testings) of Jesus by the devil (different order) |
| 5:3, 6, 4, 11–12 | 6:20b–23 | Beatitudes (different order, wording) |
| 5:44, 39b–40, 42 | 6:27–30 | Love of enemies; turn other cheek; give coat; give to beggars |
| 7:12 | 6:31 | What you wish others to do to you, do to them |
| 5:46–47, 45, 48 | 6:32–33, 15b–36 | Love more than those who love you; be merciful as the Father is |
| 7:1–2 | 6:37a, 38c | Judge not and be not judged; measure given is measure received |
| 15:14; 10:24–25a | 6:39–40 | Can blind lead the blind; disciple not above teacher |
| 7:3–5 | 6:41–42 | Speck in brother's eye, log in one's own |
| 7:16–20 (12:33–35) | 6:43–45 | No good tree bears bad fruit; no figs from thorns |
| 7:21, 24–27 | 6:46–49 | Calling me Lord and not doing; hearing my words and doing them |
| 8:5a–10, 13 | 7:1–2, 6b–10 | Centurion at Capernaum begs help for sick servant, marvelous faith |
| 11:2–11 | 7:18–28 | Disciples of JBap; the message to him; praise of JBap as more than prophet |
| 11:16–19 | 7:31–35 | This generation pleased by neither JBap nor Son of Man |
| 8:19–22 | 9:57–60 | Son of Man has nowhere to lay head; to follow him let dead bury dead |
| 9:37–38; 10:7–16 | 10:2–12 | Harvest plentiful, laborers few; mission instructions |

| MATTHEW | LUKE | CONTENTS |
|---|---|---|
| 11:21–23; 10:40 | 10:13–16 | Woe to Chorazin, Bethsaida; whoever hears you, hears me |
| 11:25–27; 13:16–17 | 10:21–24 | Thanking the Father for revealing to infants; all things given to the Son who alone knows the Father; blessed eyes that see what you see |
| 6:9–13 | 11:2–4 | The Lord's Prayer (variant forms—Matthew's longer) |
| 7:7–11 | 11:9–13 | Ask and it will be given; if you give good gifts, how much more the Father |
| 12:22–30 | 11:14–15, 17–23 | Demons cast out by Beelzebul; strong man guards his palace; not with me, against me |
| 12:43–45 | 11:24–26 | Unclean spirit gone out of someone returns and brings seven others, making worse |
| 12:38–42 | 11:29–32 | Generation seeks sign; sign of Jonah; judgment by people of Nineveh, queen of south |
| 5:15; 6:22–23 | 11:33–35 | Not putting lamp under bushel; eye lamp of body, if unsound, darkness |
| 23:25–26, 23, 6–7a, 27 | 11:39–44 | Pharisees cleanse outside of cup; woe for tithing inconsequentials, seeking first place |
| 23:4, 29–31 | 11:46–48 | Woe to lawyers for binding heavy burdens, building tombs of the prophets |
| 23:34–36, 13 | 11:49–52 | I speak/God's wisdom speaks; will send prophets who will be persecuted; woe to lawyers |
| 10:26–33; 12:32 | 12:2–10 | All covered to be revealed; fear not killers of body; acknowledging me before God |
| 10:19–20 | 12:11–12 | Before synagogues, Holy Spirit will help |
| 6:25–33 | 12:22–31 | Don't be anxious about the body; consider lilies of the field; Father knows what you need |
| 6:19–21 | 12:33–34 | No treasures on earth but in heaven |
| 24:43–44, 45–51 | 12:39–40, 42–46 | Householder and thief; faithful servant preparing for master's coming |
| 10:34–36 | 12:51–53 | Not come to bring peace but sword; divisions in family |
| 16:2–3 | 12:54–56 | Ability to interpret weather signs should enable to interpret present times |

| MATTHEW | LUKE | CONTENTS |
|---|---|---|
| 5:24–26 | 12:58–59 | Settling before going before the magistrate |
| 13:31–33 | 13:18–21 | Kingdom of heaven/God: like growth of mustard seed; like leaven woman puts in meal |
| 7:13–14, 22–23; 8:11–12 | 13:23–29 | Narrow gate through which few will enter; householder refusing those who knock; people coming from all directions to enter kingdom of heaven/God |
| 23:37–39 | 13:34–35 | Jerusalem, killing the prophets, must bless him who comes in the Lord's name |
| 22:2–10 | 14:16–24 | Kingdom of heaven/God: a great banquet, invitees make excuses, others invited |
| 10:37–38 | 14:26–27 | Anyone coming must prefer me over family and must bear a cross |
| 5:13 | 14:34–35 | Uselessness of salt that has lost its savor |
| 18:12–14 | 15:4–7 | Man who leaves 99 sheep to go after lost one |
| 6:24 | 16:13 | Cannot serve two masters |
| 11:12–13; 5:18, 32 | 16:16–18 | Law and prophets till JBap; not a dot of law will pass; divorcing wife and marrying another is adultery |
| 18:7, 15, 21–22 | 17:1, 3b–4 | Woe to tempters; forgive brother after rebuking; Peter: how often to forgive |
| 17:20 | 17:6 | If you had faith like grain of mustard seed, could move mountains |
| 24:26–28 | 17:23–24, 37 | Signs of the coming of the Son of Man |
| 24:37–39 | 17:26–27, 30 | As in the days of Noah, so will be the coming of the Son of Man |
| 10:39 | 17:33 | Whoever finds one's life will lose it; whoever loses will find it |
| 24:40–41 | 17:34–35 | On that night, of two, one taken and the other left |
| 25:14–30 | 19:12–27 | Parable of the pounds/talents |
| 19:28 | 22:38, 30 | Followers will sit on thrones judging the twelve tribes of Israel |

# 14. *M* Passages

Scholars naturally differ on assigning passages to *M*. The following list is our own.

1–2

5:19–24

5:27–28

5:33–37

6:1–8

6:16–18

7:6

10:5–6

10:23

11:1

12:36–37

13:24–30

13:36–52

14:28–31

16:17–19

17:24–27

18:16–21

18:23–25

19:11–12

20:1–16

21:4–5

22:11–14

23:2–3

23:5

23:8–10

23:15–22

23:24

23:33

25:31–46

27:3–10

27:19

27:62–66

28:11–15

28:16–20

# 15. The Gospel of Matthew: Overview

### Authorship

Although nothing in the gospel names the author, authorship is ascribed to Matthew, traditionally identified as the tax collector (9:9) who becomes an apostle (10:3). The church historian Eusebius quotes an early second-century bishop named Papias who claimed that "Matthew compiled the sayings [Gk. *logia*] in the Hebrew language, and everyone translated them as best they could" (*History of the Church*, 3.39.16). Although many of the church fathers took this to mean the gospel was originally composed in Hebrew, the canonical gospel we have, and the Gospel of Mark on which Matthew relied, existed only in Greek. One solution might be that Matthew had some kind of compilation of Aramaic or Hebrew scripture texts or sayings of Jesus for his use, but these were translated into Greek for incorporation into his gospel. Another possibility could be that Papias was referring to what modern scholars call *Q*.

### Audience

Matthew's audience is a Christian community from the Jewish tradition. They are familiar with the Old Testament to which Matthew often refers in order to illustrate its fulfillment in the person, ministry, and passion of Jesus. Matthew also expects his audience to be familiar with the Jewish Law and its ritual practices.

### Date

Most likely during the decade from AD 80 to 90. The tension between Judaism and Christianity as alternative ways of holiness began to diverge radically after the destruction of the Jerusalem temple in AD 70. By the mid-eighties, Judaism was undergoing a transformation. Christians were no longer a sect within Judaism, but something more independent.

### Community Situation

Matthew's Jewish Christian community, very likely located in the vicinity of Antioch in Syria, had come to a turning point. No longer welcome within Judaism and not yet comfortable with their role in the growing church involvement with the Gentile mission, they were struggling to find their Christian identity.

### Purpose

Matthew's gospel provides his community with a sense of who they are both as heirs of the Jewish tradition and as followers of the new way of Christian righteousness (rightly relating to God) that Jesus taught. The destruction of the Jerusalem temple was interpreted by the community as God's judgment on the Jews just as Jesus had foretold. Matthew's gospel reminds the community that they, not Pharisaic Judaism, are the true and genuine Israel. When Pharisaic Judaism expelled Matthew's community from the synagogues, they, like Paul some forty years before, decided to proclaim the gospel to the Gentiles. This decision apparently created controversy within the community. Matthew's gospel defends this direction by rooting it in the ministry of Jesus. His story is the foundational story that grounds their Christian identity and provides assurance that the direction that Matthew wants his community to follow is the right one. Remaining true both to their Jewish tradition and to the example of Jesus, the community will be prepared to carry on the mission of Jesus and "make disciples of all nations."

### Characteristics and Literary Style

Matthew's gospel adopts Mark's general gospel structure. Utilizing the *Q* source of sayings of Jesus (which Luke also uses), Matthew presents five major discourses of Jesus the teacher (chapters 5–7, 10, 13, 18, 24–25). Between the discourses, Jesus is shown in action doing the things he has talked about. Matthew also adds infancy materials focusing on Joseph as well as on resurrection narratives from his community's own traditions that reflect their distinctive theology and Christology. Matthew writes in a good but rather undistinguished Greek, more polished than that of Mark or *Q* but not as elegant as Luke. His style is didactic and generally styled for teaching. He normally tightens Mark's narratives to highlight the essential points that he wishes to teach. He is repetitive (a major feature of oral learning) and relies on many formulas and Old Testament citations, leading words, and inclusions. He is strongly influenced by the Septuagint translation of the Old Testament. He follows Mark in using doublets or triads.

### Matthean Themes

- Peter
- Church
- Sharing in Jesus' mission
- Doing rather than saying
- Continuity with Old Testament
- Mountains as a literary device
  - Christianity as the True Israel
  - Fulfillment of scriptures
  - Jesus and Old Testament figures (Moses, prophet, wisdom teacher)
  - Righteousness
  - The kingdom of heaven
- Openness to a new future
  - Jesus' death-resurrection as beginning of the final age
  - Gentiles often respond more appropriately than Jews
  - Jewish leaders consciously reject Jesus
  - Call to make disciples of all nations

### Matthew's Portrait of Jesus

- Jesus is *the* authoritative teacher, a compassionate master who proclaims, teaches, and heals as a sign of God's powerful presence in our world for salvation.
- Some important titles for Jesus are: Messiah, Son of God, Son of David, Emmanuel [God with us], King, Lord, and Son of Man.

### Matthew's Portrait of Discipleship

Answering the invitation of Jesus, disciples commit themselves in loyalty to a group that is characterized by being with Jesus to share his ministry and his suffering. The community of disciples (an *ekklesia* or church) shares a spiritual bond with Jesus that is deeper than that of family. They are characterized by their "little faith" that must grow through the process of conversion. The five major discourses of the gospel and the passion narrative are an invitation to a conversion process:

- Beginning a conversion of heart (Matt 5–7)
- Sharing in Jesus' mission (Matt 10)
- Deepening insight through parables (Matt 13)
- Directives for life as a community of disciples (Matt 18)
- Directives for life without the earthly Jesus (Matt 24–25)

### The Gospel Pattern

Matthew stresses that Jesus ushers in God's powerful rule over our world. Jesus confronts us with a choice. We must decide to follow or to reject him. Each person who responds to Jesus reflects the positive and negative possibilities of salvation.

# 16. Jesus' Journey in Matthew

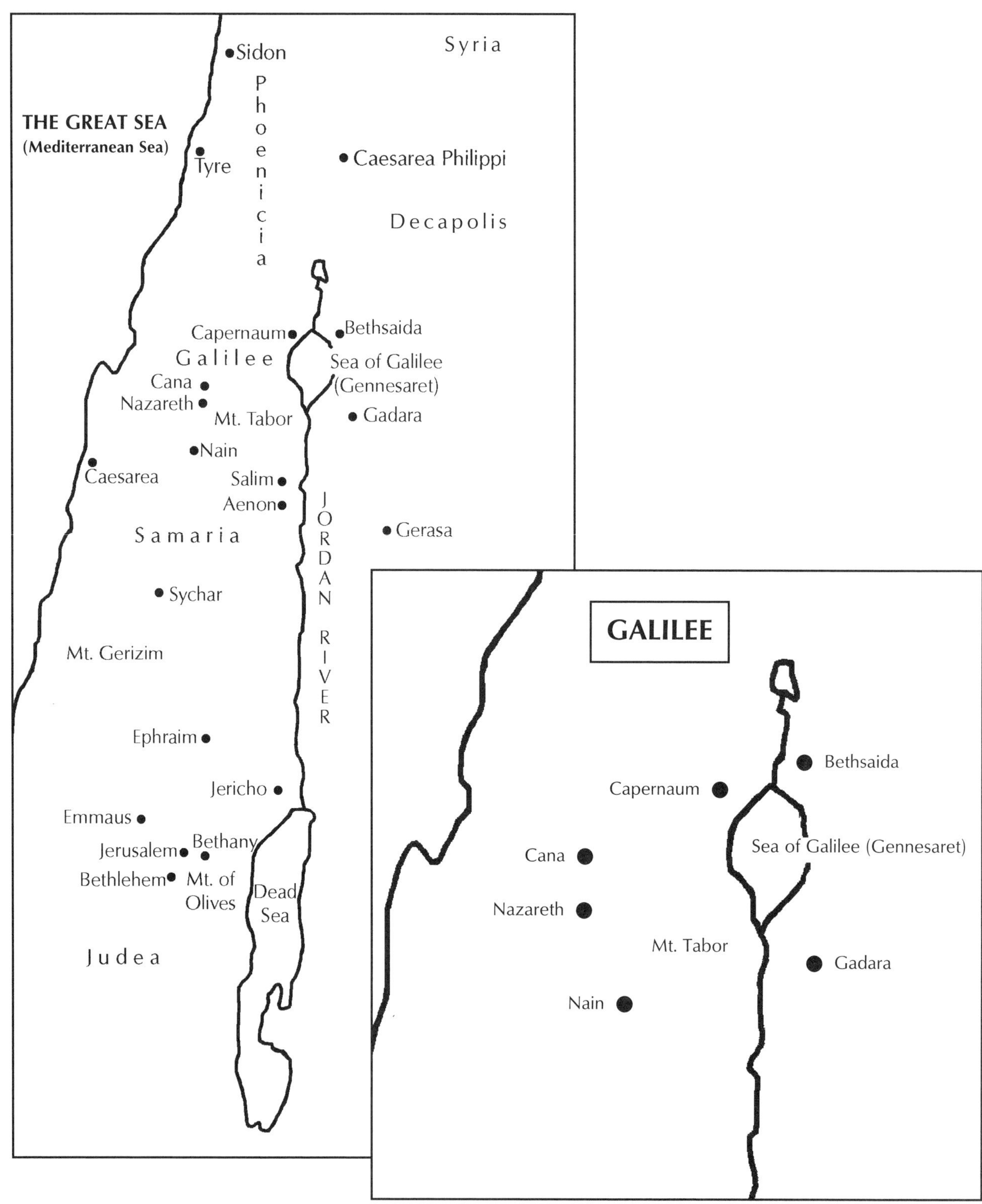

# 17. Self-Quiz: Mid-Unit Three

1. Briefly describe the structure of Matthew's gospel.

2. How would you characterize the portrait of Jesus in Matthew's gospel?

3. Briefly explain at least two important themes in Matthew's gospel.

4. How does Matthew indicate the primacy of Peter among the disciples?

5. Make sure you can locate the following places on a map:

Bethlehem
Jerusalem
Bethsaida
Capernaum
Nazareth
Caesarea Philippi
Sea of Galilee
Dead Sea
Galilee
Judea

*(Answers to quiz can be found on page 114)*

# 18. Four Ways to Follow Jesus

Steve Mueller

"Come, follow me!" With this inviting command and commanding invitation, Jesus calls followers to a Christ-like life. Through the ages every Christian has been challenged to put these words into action. Where do we go today for models of discipleship? We can learn from saints of the past or exemplary Christians today. But most importantly we must start with the basics—the four classic portraits of discipleship found in the gospels.

Like the bumper-sticker theologians who proclaim "Jesus is the Answer," the evangelists believed that Jesus was the solution to the baffling problems that their communities faced in the last thirty years of the first century. The evangelists composed their gospels to help their communities find the best way to follow Christ. They portrayed Jesus in such a way that his words and deeds became the major example of Christian living.

As you may already know, the four gospels give us four different portraits of Jesus. Taking things a step further, we now want to draw from the gospels four different ways of discipleship. We also want to show how each model or way of following Jesus can be put into practice in our times. As we explore the gospel models of discipleship, we will recall, first of all, the particular situation of the evangelists and the problems they faced. Then we will notice how each evangelist portrays Jesus as the solution to these problems.

### Following Mark's "Suffering Servant"

Mark's is the earliest written gospel. Although we can never retrieve his motives for writing, his invention of a new form for proclaiming the Christian message suggests that the old ways were no longer working. New situations demanded new solutions.

Mark wrote about the year 70, when the Romans destroyed the Jewish Temple in Jerusalem. This was a dangerous time for Christians. In Palestine, the Jewish rebellion of 66–74 shattered the peace of the Roman Empire. Jews and their Christian neighbors were treated with equal harshness. In Rome, for the first time in their history, Christians were singled out for persecution by the Emperor Nero who blamed them for the burning of Rome in 64. The Romans had always thought of Christians as a Jewish group. But now Christians could no longer hide their special identity. Did these persecutions mean that God had now abandoned Mark's Christian community?

Using Jesus as his model, Mark gives his community new answers to the urgent questions of who they are and what they must do to follow Jesus in the chaotic experience of war, persecution and apparent abandonment. The stakes are high because in the face of persecution it is much easier to deny one's Christian identity than to suffer. In this time of heightened anxiety, when old ways are ending and new directions are not yet clear, Mark shapes his gospel as the haunting story of the Messiah who suffers so others can live, whose death and apparent abandonment culminates in new life with God.

The main thrust of Mark's gospel is to identify Jesus, "the Christ, the son of God" (1:1) as the Suffering Servant of Isaiah 52:13—53:12. Throughout the first half of the gospel, Mark confirms the conventional Jewish expectations about the Messiah. Jesus appears as a prophetic teacher and lawgiver like Moses, a miracle worker like Elijah and a kingdom builder like David (although his is spiritual rather than political).

Mark then turns all of these tidy expectations on their head. Jesus is indeed the Messiah, but he "must suffer greatly, be rejected, and be killed, and rise after three days" (8:31). The rest of the gospel shows how the suffering Messiah fulfills God's plan for salvation. Mark presents the passion of Jesus as the great reversal of the common expectation that the Messiah would be a glorious king like David who would free the Jewish people from their oppressive Roman overlords. Jesus is indeed a king, but one who is crowned with thorns, mocked and beaten, and enthroned on a cross in humiliation with a sign indicating that he is "the King of the Jews." Mark's final picture of an abandoned Jesus dying alone outside the holy city challenges all the usual expectations about Jesus as a glorious and triumphant Messiah.

Mark's portrait of Jesus as the Suffering Servant of God who gives his life for all is also the clue to his portrait of genuine discipleship. What happened to Jesus will happen to us. Following Jesus means not expecting that God will save us *from* our suffering, but that God will save us *through* our suffering. The cross is the only way to the crown of new life. But Mark stresses that Jesus' way of the cross is not a dead end. Paradoxically, Jesus' way of dying is the only way to new life in God!

Throughout Christian history, Mark's model of suffering service has been especially prominent in times of religious anxiety and persecution. In Latin America Mark's model is exemplified not only by El Salvador's Archbishop Oscar Romero, who was gunned down while saying Mass, and by the brutal murders of the four American women missionaries a few months later, but also by the thousands of "disappeared" who were martyred for their commitment to faith and freedom.

Pope Paul VI was another example of suffering service. In the time of anxiety created by the changes demanded by Vatican Council II, he was caught between the new and the old, the conservatives and the progressives, tradition and innovation. Despite the suffering he absorbed from all sides, his model of cautious yet real change moved the Church in the direction indicated by the Council.

In our own families, suffering service is an essential part of parenting and family life. The demand of constant care is the sacrifice parents must make. In the first few years of life, mothers especially sacrifice sleep, time, energy and their own health so that their child might grow. Parents continue to sacrifice to provide what their children need. For any family to make it through the years, not only the parents but each member must be ready to make sacrifices, to give in sometimes, and to help one another.

### Following Matthew's "Compassionate Teacher"

Matthew revised Mark's gospel because it no longer answered the problems facing his community. By the mid-eighties of the first century, the war was over and Roman persecutions decreased. Then new problems arose for the community. Matthew's primarily Jewish community was facing marginalization in a Church that was fast becoming almost exclusively non-Jewish. Matthew realized that his community would be able to continue only if they could step out from the solid foundation of their Jewish tradition into the wider Gentile-Christian world. How could he acquaint his community with their tradition and yet urge them into the mainstream of the mainly Gentile Church? His gospel is his answer.

Matthew presents Jesus as the Master, a teacher and compassionate healer who guides us step by step through a course in Christian discipleship. The disciples are learners, which is the primary meaning of the Greek word for disciple.

Matthew's Jesus often characterizes the disciples as having "little faith" (6:30, 8:26, 14:31, 16:8, 17:20). They respond to the call of Jesus and then tag along with him—listening to his words and observing his miraculous deeds. Like us, they grow in faith as they learn about Jesus and his rigorous demands for discipleship. Becoming a disciple means not just knowing about what Jesus said and did, but putting his demands into action (7:21).

Peter serves as Matthew's example of both the positive and negative possibilities of our discipleship. The first to be called (4:18–22), Peter responds eagerly and becomes the leader of the disciples (10:2, 15:15, 17:1–8, 24–27). He responds so correctly to the question of Jesus' identity that Jesus recognizes that this profession of faith is the kind on which a church can be built (16:13–20).

Despite this great privilege, Peter is still a person of "little faith" who needs to grow. He can be the founding rock or a stumbling block. He is challenged to have faith enough to follow Jesus across water (14:20–33), to avoid being an obstacle to the passion (16:21–23), and to be a leader whose forgiveness is unlimited (18:21–35). Even the failure of Peter during the passion does not keep him from being a leader. He is one who shows the ups and downs of the discipleship challenge. Always a learner, Peter can be a model for us who know that we are far from perfect in our following of Jesus.

The risen Christ tells the disciples that their task in the world is to "make disciples of all nations" (28:18–20). They will use the gospel to teach the way of discipleship as Jesus has taught them. Being a disciple means carrying on the ministry of Jesus, becoming a Master of the Christian Way and sharing this with others so that they can become followers of Jesus.

Christian history is full of examples of compassionate teachers who have made the Church's teaching understandable so we could grow in faith. In our time, perhaps the most widely known Catholic apologist was Bishop Fulton Sheen. For over forty years, his books, radio and television shows informed both Catholics and non-Catholics about Catholicism. His lively and witty style helped millions to believe that their Catholic faith helped make life worth living.

The six martyred Jesuits of El Salvador are also examples of compassionate [discipleship]. Although we think of them as martyrs, they were college professors killed because they dared to start a university that told the truth. Driven by compassion, they approached problems from the viewpoint of the poor and offered new solutions that shattered the vested interests of the government and the military regime that oppressed the poor.

Compassionate teaching is also an essential part of parenting. The Church reminds parents that they are the primary religious educators of their children. Like Matthew's Jesus, their compassionate teaching occurs not only when children ask questions about Catholic beliefs, but also when the parents communicate Christian values by their own behavior. Kids assimilate their Christian lifesense from their parents.

### Following Luke's "Healing Witness"

Luke also set about to adapt Mark's gospel to the needs of his primarily Gentile community in the mid-eighties. Luke wanted to show that what happened with Jesus was foreshadowed in the Old Testament and continued after Jesus' death in the life of the Christian disciples. Luke tells the story of our salvation in two volumes, the Gospel and Acts of the Apostles.

Luke's very engaging portrait of Jesus focuses on his activity as a healing-saving prophet. Born "a Savior" (2:11), he comes "to seek and to save what is lost" (19:10). The ambiguity of the Greek word for save/heal allows Luke to stress that our bodily and spiritual health are interconnected. When Jesus tells those he cures, "Go, your faith has saved you," this could also mean "your faith has healed you" (7:50, 8:48, 17:19, 18:42).

Jesus' ministry of healing is God's salvation and so breaks across all our humanly created boundaries. Like a magnet, Jesus draws the poor, the outcasts, the sick, women, and foreigners to himself for healing. Through his powerful parables about the lost coin, the lost son and the lost sheep (15:1–32), Jesus challenges us to reach out beyond our narrow and comfortable borders to seek and save the lost.

Luke characterizes Jesus as a prophet, "mighty in word and deed" (24:19; see also 4:24, 7:16, 7:39). His job description (4:16-30, 7:22–23) is from the prophet Isaiah. As a spokesperson for God, Jesus' prophetic message is an invitation to see the world from God's perspective rather than from a human viewpoint. His suffering is also part of the prophet's role (13:33–34). In the passion Luke portrays Jesus as an innocent martyr. Pilate (23:4, 14, 22), Herod (23:15) and the centurion at the foot of the cross all declare him innocent (23:47). Jesus dies as he lived—forgiving his persecutors and saving a good thief.

For Luke, Mary stands out as a model of genuine discipleship. Like the prophets of old, she is characterized as a person who responds wholeheartedly to God's call. Her "Let it be" starts God's work both in her body and in her life to bring forth Jesus (1:26–38). She keeps all these things in her heart and ponders them (2:19). In the ministry of Jesus, she is identified as one who "hears the word and acts on it" (8:21). After the resurrection she is found praying in the community of disciples as they await the Pentecostal empowerment of the Holy Spirit for their mission (Acts 1:14).

Luke highlights his way of discipleship more clearly in the Acts of the Apostles. The risen Christ reveals to the disciples that the Kingdom will come through their Spirit-filled witness (1:8) to the ends of the earth. They will witness with their words and with their lives. Being a Christian demands fearless witness and a shattering of the borders between Jew and Gentile to build a new community in Christ.

When we think of Lukan discipleship, we ought to think of the many prophetic people who have called our attention to the oppression, hatred and violence that plague our society and those who have tried to break the boundaries that separate us. In the late fifties, Dr. Tom Dooley gathered worldwide cooperation in his effort to bring medical aid to the people of Vietnam and Laos long before these places were household words. Mother Theresa of Calcutta worked with the "poorest of the poor" and dared to touch the "untouchables" of the lowest class of people in India's rigid class system. And we all remember the pictures of Pope John Paul II visiting in prison and forgiving his would-be assassin.

Closer to home, the Catholic Worker Movement of Dorothy Day and Peter Maurin sensitized all of us to the problems of the poor and the need for better solutions to their problems. Martin Luther King's prophetic witness and non-violent tactics broke down many barriers of racial prejudice. Cesar Chavez gave pride and strength to Mexican-American migrant workers in their fight against injustice and exploitation.

Pope John XXIII also exemplifies Lukan discipleship. His whole life was given to breaking down the boundaries that separated Christians from one another. While in Turkey during World War II, he aided Jews fleeing Nazi persecution. As pope, he established ecumenical relationships with other churches and with secular leaders. He was the first pope ever to address an encyclical about peace on earth not only to Catholics but to all men and women of good will. His unexpected idea for Vatican Council II was a great prophetic step that unleashed the Holy Spirit to create a renewed "Church in the Modern World."

In our families, there are so many things that go wrong—addictive behaviors, abusive and dysfunctional relationships, inadequate parenting, divorce, sickness, suicide, tragic accidents, the list goes on and on. Healing witness is a constant need. Each of us is challenged to cross the boundaries of our own comfort zone to reconcile and be reconciled with others. To admit our mistakes, to say we are sorry, to forgive and be forgiven are Christian behaviors that have to be part of any family's everyday life.

### Following John's "Loving Friend"

As has often been noted, John's gospel is very different from the other three. John stresses the divine character of Jesus. Jesus is the Word, the revealer of the mystery of God in our midst. He can do this because of his personal experience and his special relationship with God. More than any other gospel, John stresses the intimate relationship of Jesus the Son to God the Father. For John, Jesus is indeed the Beloved Son of the Father.

When Jesus calls disciples, he invites them into a deep and tender experience of intimacy with him and consequently with the Father. Jesus' disciples are no longer merely pupils, but "friends" (15:15). John's community is a group conscious of its intimate relationship to Jesus, as Jesus' long discourses at the Last Supper make clear. They are a community of Jesus' friends who share the life of Jesus because they share the Holy Spirit. They are characterized by their love for one another. They are to love as Jesus has loved them—a love that is not only intimate but that gives everything for the beloved. Jesus' death is the ultimate sign of his love.

A mysterious figure appears in John's gospel. This "beloved disciple" represents John's ideal disciple. The "beloved disciple" is so intimate with Jesus that he can rest his head on Jesus at the Last Supper (13:23). In contrast to Peter, he faithfully follows Jesus during the passion, even getting Peter into the courtyard of the high priest (18:15). Although Peter denies Jesus and runs away, the beloved disciple stands at the foot of the cross (19:26). Jesus tells the beloved disciple to care for his mother. After the resurrection, the beloved disciple more quickly believes in the resurrection (20:8) and recognizes the mysterious risen Lord (21:7). He is the model of loving friendship for John's congregation.

Within our own circle of family, friends and associates are good examples of "loving friends" who will love, support and walk with us in times of trial and trouble. On the larger scene, we know of church leaders and ecumenists have been inspired by the Johannine view of fostering love and building up the Christian community "so that all might be one" (17:21). For instance, we can point to the example of Pope Paul VI openly embracing the Greek Orthodox Patriarch Athenagoras I and erasing a thousand years of hostility between the churches.

John's model has also been exemplified by spiritual writers and mystics who have influenced so many to become closer "friends" with Jesus through prayer. Thomas Merton, who turned his back on a promising career to become a Trappist monk, popularized the forgotten treasures of our spiritual tradition. His articles, books and talks helped millions to discover contemplative prayer as part of their own lives again.

John's ideal of loving friendship can help us create renewed experiences of Christian community. Beginning with our own families, we need to embrace Jesus' call to build unity. Our family experience of Church can then become the basis for a new experience of parish community in which people really know one another, pray together and reach out to others through their witness and concern. In particular, our parish life must include not only a prayerful participation in the liturgy but also involvement in the Church's work to evangelize our culture and to struggle for the common good. This local energy can, in turn, help transform the larger Church and world into a loving community.

### Our Own Way: Following Jesus Today

The four evangelists sketched ways to faithfully follow Jesus in the situations in which they found themselves. Just as their portraits of Jesus shape the contours of their ways of discipleship, so our understanding of Jesus will be the key to our way of discipleship.

Luckily for us, there are many portraits of Jesus to choose from. Since we can shape our way of discipleship from all the Jesus portraits, our personal style will probably include aspects from each of the four gospel ways.

Moreover, our way of discipleship must relate to our experience of being a Christian in the world today. Although the world has changed immensely since the time of Jesus and the early Christians, the fundamental challenges they experienced still exist.

In a changing world of powerful domination and exploitation, Mark challenges us to a way of service and self-denial that will always cost us dearly. In a world of indifference and unconcern, Matthew challenges us to a way of compassionate instruction that discovers God as our mysterious companion ("When did we see you hungry, thirsty, a stranger, naked or in prison?" Matt 25:37–40). In a world of political, racial, economic, social, geographical and religious divisions, Luke challenges us to a way of reconciling witness that breaks the boundaries we find. In a world of hatred and lonely isolation, John challenges us to a way of familiar friendship in community with God and others.

The bottom line is that there is no easy way to follow Jesus. We want our discipleship to be characterized by control over our lives, comfortable service, fixed boundaries, and easy access to God. Jesus reminds us that his way is often difficult and hard (Matt 7:14). Any way we choose to follow Jesus will demand suffering service, compassionate [discipleship], healing witness and loving friendship that we can be sure will be tested daily.

This article originally appeared as "Four Ways to Follow Jesus," *Catholic Update,* [CU 1292], published by St. Anthony Messenger Press. The article was subsequently updated by the author. Used with permission.

# 19. *Nostra Aetate* §4

## Declaration on the Relation of the Church to Non-Christian Religions, *Nostra Aetate,* Proclaimed by His Holiness Pope Paul VI on November 29, 1965

4. As the sacred synod searches into the mystery of the Church, it remembers the bond that spiritually ties the people of the New Covenant to Abraham's stock. Thus the Church of Christ acknowledges that, according to God's saving design, the beginnings of her faith and her election are found already among the Patriarchs, Moses and the prophets. She professes that all who believe in Christ—Abraham's sons according to faith[6]—are included in the same Patriarch's call, and likewise that the salvation of the Church is mysteriously foreshadowed by the chosen people's exodus from the land of bondage. The Church, therefore, cannot forget that she received the revelation of the Old Testament through the people with whom God in His inexpressible mercy concluded the Ancient Covenant. Nor can she forget that she draws sustenance from the root of that well-cultivated olive tree onto which have been grafted the wild shoots, the Gentiles.[7] Indeed, the Church believes that by His cross Christ, Our Peace, reconciled Jews and Gentiles, making both one in Himself.[8]

The Church keeps ever in mind the words of the Apostle about his kinsmen: "theirs is the sonship and the glory and the covenants and the law and the worship and the promises; theirs are the fathers and from them is the Christ according to the flesh" (Rom. 9:4–5), the Son of the Virgin Mary. She also recalls that the Apostles, the Church's mainstay and pillars, as well as most of the early disciples who proclaimed Christ's Gospel to the world, sprang from the Jewish people.

As Holy Scripture testifies, Jerusalem did not recognize the time of her visitation,[9] nor did the Jews in large number, accept the Gospel; indeed not a few opposed its spreading.[10] Nevertheless, God holds the Jews most dear for the sake of their Fathers; He does not repent of the gifts He makes or of the calls He issues—such is the witness of the Apostle.[11] In company with the Prophets and the same Apostle, the Church awaits that day, known to God alone, on which all peoples will address the Lord in a single voice and "serve him shoulder to shoulder" (Soph. 3:9).[12]

Since the spiritual patrimony common to Christians and Jews is thus so great, this sacred synod wants to foster and recommend that mutual understanding and respect which is the fruit, above all, of biblical and theological studies as well as of fraternal dialogues.

True, the Jewish authorities and those who followed their lead pressed for the death of Christ;[13] still, what happened in His passion cannot be charged against all the Jews, without distinction, then alive, nor against the Jews of today. Although the Church is the new people of God, the Jews should not be presented as rejected or accursed by God, as if this followed from the Holy Scriptures. All should see to it, then, that in catechetical work or in the preaching of the word of God they do not teach anything that does not conform to the truth of the Gospel and the spirit of Christ.

Furthermore, in her rejection of every persecution against any man, the Church, mindful of the patrimony she shares with the Jews and moved not by political reasons but by the Gospel's spiritual love, decries hatred, persecutions, displays of anti-Semitism, directed against Jews at any time and by anyone.

Besides, as the Church has always held and holds now, Christ underwent His passion and death freely, because of the sins of men and out of infinite love, in order that all may reach salvation. It is, therefore, the burden of the Church's preaching to proclaim the cross of Christ as the sign of God's all-embracing love and as the fountain from which every grace flows.

### Notes

6. Cf. *Gal.* 3:7.
7. Cf. *Rom.* 11:17–24.
8. Cf. *Eph.* 2:14–16.
9. Cf. *Lk.* 19:44.
10. Cf. *Rom.* 11:28.
11. Cf. *Rom.* 11:28–29; cf. Dogmatic Constitution, *Lumen Gentium* (Light of nations) AAS, 57 (1965) p. 20.
12. Cf. *Is.* 66:23; *Ps.* 65:4; *Rom.* 11:11–32.
13. Cf. *John* 19:6.

# 20. The Jewish People and Their Sacred Scriptures in the Christian Bible

## The Pontifical Biblical Commission

### III. B. 1. *The Gospel according to Matthew*

The relationship between the First Gospel and the Jewish world is extremely close. Many details in it show a great familiarity with the Scriptures, the traditions and the mentality of the Jewish milieu. More than Mark and Luke, Matthew stresses the Jewish origin of Jesus: the genealogy presents him as "son of David, son of Abraham" (Mt 1:1) and goes no further back. The etymology of Jesus' name is underlined: the child of Mary will bear this name "because it is he who will save his people from their sins" (1:21). Jesus' mission during his public life is limited "to the lost sheep of the house of Israel" (15:24), and he assigns the same limits to the mission of the Twelve (10:5–6). More than the other evangelists, Matthew often takes care to note that events in Jesus' life happened "so that what had been spoken through the prophets might be fulfilled" (2:23). Jesus himself makes it clear that he has come not to abolish the Law, but to fulfill it (5:17).

Nevertheless, it is clear that the Christian communities kept their distance from the Jewish communities that did not believe in Jesus Christ. A significant detail: Matthew does not say that Jesus taught "in *the* synagogues," but "in *their* synagogues" (4:23; 9:35; 13:54), in this way noting the separation. Matthew introduces two of the three Jewish parties described by the historian Josephus, the Pharisees and the Sadducees, but always in a context of opposition to Jesus. This is also true for the scribes,[313] who are frequently associated with the Pharisees. Another significant fact: it is in the first prediction of the passion (16:21) that the three divisions of the Sanhedrin, "the elders, chief priests and scribes," make their first appearance together in the Gospel. They are also set in a situation of radical opposition to Jesus.

Jesus many times confronts the opposition of the scribes and Pharisees, and finally responds by a vigorous counter-offensive (23:2–7, 13–36) where the phrase "Scribes and Pharisees, hypocrites!" occurs six times. This invective certainly reflects, in part at least, the situation of Matthew's community. The redactional context is that of two groups living in close contact with one another: Jewish Christians, convinced that they belong to authentic Judaism, and those Jews who do not believe in Christ Jesus, considered by Christians to be unfaithful to their Jewish vocation in their docility to blind and hypocritical guides.

It should be noted that Matthew's polemic does not include Jews in general. These are not named apart from the expression "the King of the Jews," applied to Jesus (2:2; 27:11, 29, 37) and in the final chapter (28:15), a phrase of minor importance. The polemic is for the most part internal, between two groups both belonging to Judaism. On the other hand, only the leaders are in view. Although in Isaiah's message the whole vine is reprimanded (Is 5:1–7), in Matthew's parable it is only the tenants who are accused (Mt 21:33–41). The invective and the accusations hurled at the scribes and Pharisees are similar to those found in the prophets, and correspond to a contemporary literary genre which was common in Judaism (for example, Qumran) and also in Hellenism. Moreover, they put Christians themselves on guard against attitudes incompatible with the Gospel (23:8–12).

Furthermore, the anti-Pharisee virulence of Mt 23 must be seen in the context of the apocalyptic discourse of Mt 24–25. Apocalyptic language is employed in times of persecution to strengthen the capacity for resistance on the part of the persecuted minority, and to reinforce their hopes of a liberating divine intervention. Seen in this perspective, the vigor of the polemic is less astonishing.

Nevertheless, it must be recognized that Matthew does not always confine his polemics to the leading class. The diatribe of Mt 23 against the scribes and Pharisees is followed by an apostrophe addressed to Jerusalem. It is the whole city that is accused of "killing the prophets" and of "stoning those sent to it" (23:37), and it is for the whole city that punishment is predicted (23:38). Of its magnificent Temple "there will not remain a stone upon a stone" (24:2). Here is a situation parallel to Jeremiah's time (Jer 7:26). The prophet announced the destruction of the Temple and the ruin of the city (26:6, 11). Jerusalem is about to become "a curse for all the nations of the earth" (26:6), exactly the opposite of the blessing promised to Abraham and his descendants (Gn 12:3; 22:18).

71. At the time of the Gospel's redaction, the greater part of the Jewish population had followed their leaders in their refusal to believe in Christ Jesus. Jewish Christians were only a minority. The evangelist, therefore, foresees that Jesus' threats were about to be fulfilled. These threats were not directed at Jews as Jews, but only insofar as they were in solidarity with their leaders in their lack of docility to God. Matthew expresses this solidarity in the passion narrative when he reports that at the instigation of the chief priests and elders "the crowd" demands of Pilate that Jesus be crucified (Mt 27:20–23). In response to the Roman governor's denial of responsibility, "all the people" present themselves took responsibility for putting Jesus to death (27:24–25). On the people's side, adopting this position certainly showed their conviction that Jesus merited death, but to the evangelist, such conviction was unjustifiable: the blood of Jesus was "innocent blood" (27:4), as even Judas recognized. Jesus would have made his own the words of Jeremiah: "Know for certain that if you put me to death, you will be bringing innocent blood upon yourselves and upon this city and its inhabitants" (Jer 26:15). From an Old Testament perspective, the sins of the leaders inevitably bring disastrous consequences for the whole community. If the Gospel was redacted after 70 A.D., the evangelist knew that, like Jeremiah's prediction, Jesus' prediction had also been fulfilled. But he did not see this fulfillment as final, for all the Scriptures attest that after the divine sanction God always opens up a positive perspective.[314] The discourse of Mt 23 does end on a positive note. A day will come when Jerusalem will say: "Blessed is he who comes in the name of the Lord" (23:39). Jesus' passion itself opens up the most positive perspective of all, for, from his "innocent blood" criminally shed, Jesus has constituted a "blood of the covenant," "poured out for the remission of sins" (26:38).

Like the people's cry in the passion narrative (27:25), the ending of the parable of the tenants seems to indicate that, at the time of the Gospel's composition, the majority of the Jews had followed their leaders in their refusal to believe in Jesus. Indeed, having predicted that "the kingdom of God will be taken away from you," Jesus did not add that the kingdom would be given "to other leaders," but would be given "to a *nation* producing its fruits" (21:43). The expression "a nation" is implicitly opposed to the "people of Israel"; this assuredly suggests that a great number of the subjects will not be of Jewish origin. The presence of Jews is in no way excluded, for the

Gospel community is aware that this "nation" will be set up under the authority of the Twelve, in particular of Peter, and the Twelve are Jews. With these and other Jews "many will come from east and west and will eat with Abraham and Isaac and Jacob in the kingdom of heaven, while the heirs of the kingdom will be thrown into outer darkness" (8:11–12). This universal outlook is definitively confirmed at the end of the Gospel, for the risen Jesus commands the "eleven disciples" to go and teach "all the nations" (28:19). This ending, at the same time, confirms the vocation of Israel, for Jesus is a son of Israel and in him the prophecy of Daniel concerning Israel's role in history is fulfilled. The words of the risen One: "All authority in heaven and on earth has been given to me"[315] make explicit in what sense the universal vision of Daniel and the other prophets are henceforth to be understood.

***Conclusion.*** More than the other Synoptic Gospels, Matthew is the Gospel of fulfillment—Jesus has not come to abolish, but to fulfill—for it insists more on the continuity with the Old Testament, basic for the idea of fulfillment. It is this aspect that makes possible the establishment of fraternal bonds between Christians and Jews. But on the other hand, the Gospel of Matthew reflects a situation of tension and even opposition between the two communities. In it Jesus foresees that his disciples will be flogged in the synagogues and pursued from town to town (23:34). Matthew therefore is concerned to provide for the Christians' defense. Since that situation has radically changed, Matthew's polemic need no longer interfere with relations between Christians and Jews, and the aspect of continuity can and ought to prevail. It is equally necessary to say this in relation to the destruction of the city and the Temple. This downfall is an event of the past which henceforth ought to evoke only deep compassion. Christians must be absolutely on their guard against extending responsibility for it to subsequent generations of Jews, and they must remind themselves that after a divine sanction, God never fails to open up positive new perspectives.

313. This observation is valid for the plural, not for the singular in 8:19 and 13:52.

314. Is 8:23—9:6; Jer 31–32; Ezk 36:16–38.

315. Mt 28:18; cf. Dn 7:14, 18, 27.

# 21. New Testament Writings: Overview

**PASTORAL LETTERS:**
***(1 and 2 Timothy, Titus)***

**PASTORAL**

**P ROBLEMS**
**A ND**
**S OLUTIONS**
**T HEOLOGY**
**O RGANIZATION**
**R ULES FOR BEHAVIOR**
**A TTITUDES**
**L ITURGY**

## 1 and 2 TIMOTHY, TITUS

**Date:** ca. AD 65–110

**Purpose:** To structure the community emerging in the Hellenistic world

**Themes:**
- Church = "household of God"
- Ministry/hierarchy (1 Tim)
- Faith is sound doctrine
- Guidelines for behavior
- Paul's farewell message (2 Tim)

**CATHOLIC LETTERS:**
***(James, Jude, 1 and 2 Peter, 1, 2, and 3 John)***

**CATHOLIC**

**C ONCERNS**
**A BOUT**
**T RADITION**
**H ETERODOXY (FALSE DOCTRINE/WORSHIP)**
**O RTHODOXY (TRUE DOCTRINE/WORSHIP)**
**L ITURGY**
**I NSTITUTIONS**
**C HRISTOLOGY**

## JAMES

**Date:** ca. AD 60–100

**Purpose:** To offer words of encouragement with a practical, wisdom tone

**Themes:**
- Faith and good works
- Temptation/testing
- Wisdom
- Wealth/poverty
- Right use of speech
- Genuine love of others in deeds
- Anointing of sick (5:14)
- Call to patience

## JUDE

**Date:** ca. AD 60–90

**Purpose:** To challenge believers to fight for the faith and avoid false teachers

**Themes:**
- Dangers of false teachers
- Use of Old Testament for warning
- Quotes from apocryphal books
- Faith is body of true doctrine

## 1 PETER

**Date:** ca. AD 60–90

**Purpose:** To encourage a sense of "belonging" and Jewish heritage

**Themes:**
- "Rebirth," conversion
- Baptismal commitment and dignity
- Christian suffering
- Not aliens but at home in the Church
- Peter as exhorting elder
- Church built of "living stones"
- Witness value of authentic Christian life

## 2 PETER

**Date:** ca. AD 100–125

**Purpose:** An exhortation to faith and genuine doctrine

**Themes:**
- Peter's farewell message
- Christian virtue (1:3–21)
- Warnings against false teachers (2:1–22)
- Reflections on delay of Parousia
- Uses letter of Jude as source
- Knows "all" the letters of Paul and problems of interpreting them (3:14–16)

## HEBREWS

**Date:** ca. AD 75–95

**Purpose:** To combat waning enthusiasm and nostalgia for Jewish liturgy; to enlighten and encourage

**Themes:**
- Use of Old Testament typology
- Stress on divinity and humanity of Christ
- Guidelines for a period of transition
- Jesus as new High Priest in heaven

# Self-Quiz Answers

## SELF-QUIZ: MID-UNIT ONE

1. a. Job
   b. Habakkuk
   c. Proverbs
   d. Habakkuk
   e. Job
   f. Proverbs
   g. Job
   h. Proverbs

2. Solomon

## CANON QUIZ

1. T
2. F
3. T
4. T
5. F
6. F
7. T
8. T
9. In any order:
   1 and 2 Maccabees
   Judith
   Wisdom of Solomon
   Baruch
   Tobit
   Sirach (Ecclesiasticus)
10. LXX, the Roman numeral for 70 (Septuagint)
11. Canon
12. Deuterocanonical
13. Apocrypha
14. Pseudepigrapha
15. Septuagint
16. Jamnia
17. Greek
18. Hebrew, Greek
19. | | |
    |---|---|
    | Canonical | Canonical |
    | Deuterocanonical | Apocryphal |
    | Canonical | Canonical |
    | Deuterocanonical | Apocryphal |
    | Pseudepigraphal | Pseudepigraphal |
20. Hellenistic

## SELF-QUIZ: MID-UNIT TWO

1. a. 1 Maccabees
   b. Tobit
   c. Baruch
   d. Jonah
   e. 2 Maccabees
   f. Jonah
   g. Tobit
   h. Esther
   i. Esther
   j. 2 Maccabees

2. The answer would include a brief summary of the story of Esther (for Purim) or the story of the rededication of the temple (for Hanukkah).

3. See the overview in Supplementary Reading #7 for assistance with this answer.

4. See EDB article on Hellenism for assistance with this answer.

## SELF-QUIZ: MID-UNIT THREE

1. Matthew adopts Mark's general gospel structure. Utilizing the Q source of sayings of Jesus, the evangelist presents five major discourses of Jesus the teacher (Matt 5–7; 10; 13; 18; 24–25). Between the discourses, Jesus is shown in action doing the things he has talked about. Matthew also adds an infancy narrative focusing on Joseph as well as on resurrection narratives from his community's own traditions that reflect its distinctive theology and Christology.

2. Jesus is the fulfillment of Old Testament prophecies. He is the authoritative teacher, a compassionate master who proclaims, teaches, and heals as a sign of God's powerful presence in our world for salvation. Some important titles for Jesus are: Messiah, Son of God, Son of David, Emmanuel [God with us], King, Lord, and Son of Man.

3. Possibilities include: Christianity as the true Israel; the fulfillment of scripture; continuity with the Old Testament; new righteousness; the kingdom of heaven; primacy of Peter; Jesus' death and resurrection as the beginning of the final age; non-Jews often responding more appropriately than Jews to Jesus; Jewish leaders consciously rejecting Jesus; disciples' call to share in the mission of Jesus; followers of Jesus making disciples of all nations.

4. Possibilities include: Jesus calls him "Rock" and gives him the keys to the kingdom.

## FOUR-YEAR PLAN OF STUDY IN THE CATHOLIC BIBLICAL SCHOOL

| UNITS | BIBLICAL BOOKS | THEOLOGICAL THEMES | GENERAL ISSUES |
|---|---|---|---|
| **FIRST YEAR: OLD TESTAMENT FOUNDATIONS — GENESIS THROUGH KINGS** | | | |
| **UNIT 1** | Exodus<br>Leviticus<br>Numbers | People of God<br>Covenant<br>Desert | Sources of the Pentateuch |
| **UNIT 2** | Deuteronomy<br>Genesis | Promise/The Land<br>Creation/Sin | Form Criticism<br>Fertile Crescent |
| **UNIT 3** | Joshua<br>Judges<br>1 & 2 Samuel<br>1 & 2 Kings | Charismatic Leadership<br>Kingship<br>Prophecy | Geography of Palestine<br>Canaanite Religion<br>Biblical Chronology<br>Biblical Archeology |
| **SECOND YEAR: NEW TESTAMENT FOUNDATIONS — JESUS AND DISCIPLESHIP** | | | |
| **UNIT 1** | Mark<br>Luke<br>Matthew 1 and 2 | Discipleship<br>Holy Spirit<br>Infancy Narratives | Synoptic Question<br>Form Criticism<br>Redaction Criticism |
| **UNIT 2** | Acts<br>Pauline Letters | Church<br>Gifts of the Holy Spirit | New Testament Geography<br>Letter as Literary Form |
| **UNIT 3** | John and Johannine Letters<br>Mark 13, Luke 21<br>Matthew 24–25<br>Revelation | Sacraments<br>Eschatology | Apocalyptic Writing |
| **THIRD YEAR: OLD TESTAMENT CONTINUED — EXILE AND RESTORATION** | | | |
| **UNIT 1** | Amos<br>Hosea<br>1 Isaiah<br>Micah<br>Zephaniah<br>Nahum<br>Jeremiah | Social Justice<br>Prophetic Vocation<br>Marriage of God and Israel | Biblical Chronology |
| **UNIT 2** | Lamentations<br>Obadiah<br>Ezekiel<br>2 Isaiah<br>Haggai<br>Zechariah 1–8<br>3 Isaiah<br>Ezra<br>Nehemiah | Destruction of the Temple<br><br>Meaning of the Exile<br><br>Renewal after Exile<br>Community Rebuilt around the Word | Crisis of the Exile<br>Strategies of Renewal |
| **UNIT 3** | 1 & 2 Chronicles<br>Joel<br>Malachi<br>Ruth<br>Song of Songs<br>Psalms | Rebuilding a People<br>Importance of the Law | Historical Writings of Old Testament<br><br><br>Hebrew Poetry<br>Jewish Liturgy |
| **FOURTH YEAR: THE OLD AND NEW TESTAMENTS CONCLUDED — THE WORD IN THE HELLENISTIC WORLD** | | | |
| **UNIT 1** | Proverbs<br>Habakkuk<br>Job<br>Ecclesiastes<br>Sirach<br>Wisdom | Creation Emphasis<br><br>Problem of Suffering | Priest, Prophet, and Sage |
| **UNIT 2** | Jonah<br>Esther<br>Tobit<br>Baruch<br>1 and 2 Maccabees<br>Judith<br>Daniel | Martyrdom<br><br>Resurrection | Deuterocanonical Books<br>Hellenism |
| **UNIT 3** | Matthew<br>Pastoral Letters<br>Catholic Letters<br>Hebrews | Role of Peter/Apostles<br>New Testament as Fulfillment of Old Testament | Christianity as a New Form of Religion in the Roman World |